ABOUT THE AUTHOR

Dr Michael O'Connell is a lecturer in social psychology at University College Dublin. His research interests are in the areas of inter-group relations, media representations, crime and social deprivation. He has published papers in leading journals as well as co-editing two recent books: *Crime and Poverty in Ireland* (Round Hall, Sweet and Maxwell, 1998) and *Cultivating Pluralism* (Oak Tree Press, 2000).

Changed Utterly

Ireland and the New Irish Psyche

Michael O'Connell

The Liffey Press

Published by The Liffey Press
307 Clontarf Road,
Dublin 3, Ireland

A catalogue record of this book is
available from the British Library.

ISBN 1-86076-222-0

The painting on the cover is *Collecting Meteorites at Knowth, Irelantis*
by Sean Hillen, and is the copyright of the artist, © Sean Hillen.
Reproduced here with the kind permission of the artist.

Printed in the Republic of Ireland by Colour Books Ltd.

Contents

Acknowledgements

I would like to thank the following people who gave me advice in the course of writing this book: John Browne, Alan Carr, Tom Crean, Jackie Durcan, Seamus Fitzpatrick, Ciara Goggin, Alastair Green, Eilis Hennessy, Maria Horgan, Geraldine Moane, Aidan Moran, Michael O'Toole, Noel Rowland, Anthony Whelan, Diana Caffrey and Eoin Lonergan. Of course, all errors in interpreting their advice remain the responsibility of the author.

Psychology students at UCD raised various pertinent points relevant to Irish society during many of my lectures with them and I am extremely grateful to them as well as to Wendy van Zutphen who provided very capable research support while a visiting student at UCD. I would also like to thank Ciarán Benson for substantial encouragement and advice throughout the writing process.

James McBride, Director of the Irish Social Science Data Archive at UCD, facilitated efficient access to comprehensive opinion poll data.

Pauline Grace was a source of endless ideas and resolutions to apparently intractable problems as well as providing unwavering support during the research.

And finally, this book would not have appeared without the professionalism of David Givens and Brian Langan at The Liffey Press.

To my parents

Chapter 1

NEW IRELAND?

Who Dares to Write about Contemporary Ireland?

Towards the close of the last decade of the twentieth century, three eminent British men of letters went public with their views on the meanings of Britishness and Englishness. Jeremy Paxman published his book, *The English*; Andrew Marr presented a series of television discussion programmes on the future of the United Kingdom; and Julian Barnes was shortlisted for the Booker Prize with his novel *England, England*. None of these attempts to define the meaning of Britishness was tremendously successful but this is perhaps beside the point. One could say that the very fact that they contemplated the issue turned out to be more interesting than the fruits of their contemplation. All at once, three middlebrow British intellectuals converged in their consideration about national identity (and one might also include here Norman Davies' provocative history of *The Isles* published in 1999).

No doubt, students of political life might have seen it coming — political change and increasing autonomy for the Celtic fringe of the United Kingdom inevitably triggered questions about nationhood and the Union. An impending switch of the first digit of every year from 1 to 2 added a little millenarian spice to these considerations. But the timing is still surprising. The nation-changing years in Britain were surely the Thatcher era — the society she inherited and the society she bequeathed were so entirely different that the distance between 1979 and 1990 felt much more than its 11 years. The contrast with Ireland could not be more extreme. The 1980s here were like the 1970s, only more so. Change was painfully slow and gradual in those decades while, by contrast, Ireland in the 1990s changed qualitatively, remorselessly, hungrily. It is not an exaggeration to say that a Martian leaving Ireland in 1989 and returning in 2001 would not recognise a society altered so fundamentally (although, in passing, it is worth wondering why a Martian, having seen the country in 1989, would bother returning for another look).

But there's the paradox: a British society that has long passed the white heat of change generates numerous analyses of its "new" nature at the end of the 1990s. On the other hand, Ireland, despite the whirlwind of the 1990s, sees few prominent public figures emerge with their accounts of social change or questions about a new identity or set of values. Unlike the Paxmans and Marrs of the UK, there has been little appetite to take on or reflect upon the changing character of "Irishness". (I mention a few of the honourable exceptions below.)

Yet the rapidity of that change can surely not be doubted and one of the main purposes of this book is to chart its development. Ruth Dudley Edwards has written of the Irish tendency to swing full-circle, in such a way that old and treasured icons become reviled and detested while the new and radical are accepted unquestioningly. This process of "full-circle change" cannot but conjure up the countries of Eastern Europe and their quiet anti-communist revolutions. It is pushing it somewhat, but there are some uncanny similarities. The Russians sought to abandon a state-planned collectivised economy and establish a free-market society in a 500-day session of shock therapy. In Eastern Europe more generally, the old political leaderships, who once enjoyed the kind of standing ovations that would put British Tory party conferences to shame, were hunted down, largely through constitutional methods, by the zealous new political rulers. And the statues of the secular saint Lenin came crashing to the ground all over the former USSR.

How does change in Ireland compare? While we still have not had the nerve to kick over our sacred icons of the Virgin Mary, even moving statues look a lot steadier now under our profane gaze. A once-adored section of our former political elite are reviled and discredited, and are currently being hunted through the courts and tribunals. In 1991, Richard Branson's Virgin Megastore in the centre of Dublin was pursued by the Gardaí for making condoms available for sale. Now we would happily wear condoms on our head in public if we felt it was the fashionable thing to do.

The comparison is forced, but you get the point. The degree of change in Ireland in so many domains — economic, political, religious — is difficult to fathom. And one hears it spoken of everywhere. The priorities of the 1990s were work and economic success. And we focused completely on it, to the exclusion of virtually all else. But now, having achieved some security in matters of growth (although it's a security that looks increasingly insecure), individuals have an opportunity to look around once more, a little perplexed and confused. What kind of people have we become? What are our priorities? And are they still the best fit in changing circumstances? The question is now asked frequently because rapid change has made it at once more relevant but also less easy to answer. And unlike Britain, there's little help from our intellectuals, since so few writers here have grappled directly and fully with how material success has changed the national psyche. Books have appeared but these still deal with quirky Ireland, such as John Waters' *Intelligent Person's Guide to Modern Ireland* (1997). Kerrigan and Brennan (1999) made some telling points about the corruption of the country with their A–Z of scandals in *This Great Little Nation*. An outsider like John Ardagh (1995) can describe the country so well and yet one feels certain absences in his account. Politicians have written intelligently about the country (Hussey, 1993) or its economy (MacSharry and others — see Chapter 3). In *Being Irish* (Logue, 2000), many public figures reflected thoughtfully on the general nature of Irish identity. However, most of these still fail to capture the universal but elusive theme of change — the difference between the way we live now and how things used to be. Ann Marie Hourihane's *She Moves through the Boom* (2000) was regarded by many as one of the most successful attempts at describing the characteristics of the New Ireland. Yet the shrewdness and subtlety of her descriptive style did not easily lend themselves to firm conclusions.

Academic researchers have possibly had the most to say. A key text was provided by some of the best and brightest researchers from the ESRI in their 1990 book, *Understanding Contemporary Ireland.* It showed great intelligence and an admirable breadth of scholarship. But despite being written by arguably Ireland's smartest thinkers a little over a decade ago, it now feels intensely dated. This was not the fault of the authors but the country — Ireland refused to stand still, and while sociological theory, like its dismal cousin economics, can explain the past, it is very poor at charting the future. Thus, all the pessimistic analyses of social classes and the fixed nature of Irish society appeared in this book just when a rocket was being placed under the Irish economy and social values.

There are more up-to-date accounts by sociologists like Michel Peillon and Eamonn Slater (1998/2000) and political scientists like William Crotty and David Schmitt (1998). The relative recency of their accounts and those of their contributors are useful in that one gets a sense not so much of a modernising Ireland (as anguished over in so many texts since the 1970s) but of a post-modernising Ireland. Michel Peillon cites the sociologist Anthony Giddens when he argues that Ireland's transition has been from traditionalism to simple modernity to high modernity. These concepts can be understood in shorthand as a transition from communities relying on trust and kinship to a society ruled by technical experts and ultimately to a population no longer willing to readily believe its experts and institutions. This may be as good a model as any in understanding public dismay at the scandals as diverse as those involving blood transfusion, sexual abuse and urban planning. Kieran Allen's (2000) book, a critical account of the nature of the Celtic Tiger, is written from a Marxist perspective. His assessment is an important, if partly flawed, attempt to deconstruct the ideological illusions underpinning modern Ireland and his claims are examined in Chapters 3 and 8.

Synthesis versus Analysis

Perhaps one of the most fascinating areas of change is detailed in the book edited by Christopher Whelan, *Values and Social Change in Ireland* (1994). It is certainly of substantial interest to a social psychologist since the focus is on social attitudes. The evidence used in the book is drawn from two consecutive European Values Surveys carried out ten years apart (1980 and 1990) and thus provides a barometer of change in Irish social values. There are very sharp shifts and "substantial change" recorded in certain areas such as attitudes towards women in the workplace, faith in state institutions, and moral absolutism. Less definitive and more nuanced transformations had occurred in relation to other domains such as adherence to Catholicism, trust in others and job satisfaction. I believe that these observations capture some of the complexity of conceptualising social change. There are, as is obvious, many different trends to note, often moving in contradictory directions. One might want to examine them separately, as Whelan and his co-authors have done, without attempting to impose a common model or unified path. However, an argument can be made for synthesis as well as analysis. That is, one should try to make assessments precisely and clearly in multiple ways but one should also try to link this multiplicity or range of measures and integrate them (see below for a further defence of this "integrationist" position). It is in this spirit that I will at times refer to the "Irish psyche" throughout the text, by which is meant an amalgamation or average set of Irish values. One might just as easily have used the term "national character" or even Jungian "collective unconscious" if it were not for their creepy blood and soil connotations. Let me make it clear that the use of the term "psyche" should not be taken to imply that all Irish people are the same as one another and differ from all other nations or societies — no doubt some Irish people have more in common with some British or French or Russian or Nigerian people than with each other. These intra-national differences are not denied and indeed will be explored to a certain degree in the book (see Chapters 10 and 11 for example). However, it is still legitimate to seek out the typical outlook or majority set of values and examine their change.

As well as adding synthesis to analysis, this book differs from the approach of researchers like Whelan and others in its acceptance that the author's own position is neither value-free nor value-neutral. Of course one attempts to be objective, impartial and disinterested in researching and writing around social science topics. As skilled social scientists, Whelan and his co-workers have presented a text that coolly describes survey data gathered from a representative sample of Irish people without passing judgement on their findings. However, sometimes one cannot be neutral on a theme that interests one greatly. The choice then is either not to write about it or to come clean about one's own biases. My own view, and the reader may wish to take this into account, is that Ireland desperately required social change and was a deeply unattractive society in the 1980s. On the more specific issue of what the late great boom of the last decade has done to, and for, the Irish psyche and whether, overall, it has been a "good" thing, the reader may be relieved to know that my feeling is the complexity of the debate must make any unambiguous answer to this question facile and overly simplistic. It is hoped that a reasonable analysis at the right level will be proffered, but ultimately this is simply a personal reflection on reliable data gathered by others. When, in places, my own interpretations of sets of data feel dubious, simply ignore them and trust the data.

Writing about Change

My primary sense in reflecting on Ireland today is one of surprise, perhaps amazement, at the rapidity of social transformation. Psychologically trained readers will be aware of a technique known as Osgood's semantic differential. It uses antonyms or opposites to measure how people feel about a certain social object. Examples of antonyms might be kind–cruel, good–bad, beautiful–ugly and so on. It strikes me that Ireland has changed so much in the last number of decades that the antonyms one would have chosen to evaluate this country in, say, 1981 are the opposite of those of the year 2001. So while one might have described the Ireland of the past as stagnant, poor, religious, traditional or withdrawn, now opposing adjectives spring to mind — dynamic, wealthy, secular, brash, vulgar. And it's interesting to note that the new words that spring to mind (mine at least) are not unreservedly good. Rather — and this is the nub of it — there is much ambiguity surrounding the question of where we've gone and the direction in which we've developed.

Two social processes have partly overlapped in Ireland in the last two decades: one is a general modernisation, with its greater individualism and secularism; and the other is a tremendous surge in economic growth, with its spiralling materialism, consumerism and increased choice. And the impulse to write this book arose from the sense that people were generally pleased with the evolution of the society, except for . . . And that's the thing, the "except for". It's hard to put your finger on it, but the perception is of a lingering sense of ambiguity and a vague sense of unease, despite the success. It is as though we're enjoying the pithivier of pigeon with fondant of kumquat but wonder . . . maybe the bacon and cabbage tasted better? Or indeed, could we still make bacon and cabbage if we needed to? The journalist, Tom Humphries, captured this sensation very nicely: "Everywhere you go in this frantic boom time one is struck by the sense that we as a people are losing as much as we gain; that prosperity is driving us across the plains to some place that's as likely to be an abattoir as it is to be a paradise" (*Irish Times*, 20 January 2001).

Is the price of modernity and economic success the loss of who we are as a nation? The contemporary comic auld Dublin character "Ding Dong Denny O'Reilly" has satirised this fear with his complaint that the Irish have abandoned their traditional pastimes of spittin', fightin' the Brits and incest. But as with most humour (even that in bad taste), a serious social concern is lurking within. And this is the belief, widely felt if less often explicitly stated, that the cost of modernisation and economic success and a hegemonic bland liberal consensus is the loss of identity and character, and a sense of who we are. And if our traditional morality looks a little less lustrous in the light of what we know today about the past, nonetheless some people would argue that even a dodgy traditional Catholic morality is better than no morality at all.

This debate is not entirely new, of course, since Ireland has been "modernising" since the 1960s and had enjoyed some brief if not spectacular spurts of economic growth prior to the 1990s. The sociologist Hugh Brody published his book *Inishkillane* in 1973 about life in the rural west; the same brooding tensions between modernity versus community, prosperity versus distinctiveness, emerge. The inhabitants of the village he describes, while welcoming new material comforts, rued the temporary disappearance of the old community and its network of relationships. This is a microcosm of the fears and concerns of today. The disappearance of unemployment, the decline in forced emigration and the rising wages are very welcome, but do they necessarily imply the loss of Irishness and Irish culture and the creation of a fifty-first American state or (apparently an even worse fate) the transformation of Dublin into something like a northern English city? In a typically Irish way of course, we yearn to have our cake and eat it too, to out-produce the Germans in the morning, make a killing on the stock market in the afternoon, enjoy a sweaty game of hurling in the evening before riverdancing home after a *seisiún* in the pub at night. But that does not seem possible. A psychology professor from University College Dublin understood this dilemma in 1963, when he stated presciently: "One cannot radically change the material culture and hope to preserve all the rest intact" (E.F. O'Doherty, quoted in Ardagh, 1995, p. 276). And the quiet ambiguity that people feel about change in this country suggests that they are also aware that there's no going back.

The Book Structure

The purpose of this book is thus hopefully a little clearer — to make sense of the "New Irish Psyche". And in order to do that, it is of course essential to define the "old" Irish psyche. In Chapter 2, the writings of both historians and shrewd observers of our society are briefly described so as to make a claim about the kind of people we *were*. The values, outlooks and ideologies of previous times are summarised partly because they are interesting in their own right but mainly because they are instructive about the different kind of society we live in today. There is no suggestion that people wish to return to a past scarred by the misery of economic failure and Catholic church dogmatism. On the contrary, I would argue that few regret the great advances the economy has made in recent times. While some worry how evenly the economic pie is shared, not even Green or leftist thinkers want to see it diminished. The buoyant returns for the exchequer meant that government departments had the opportunity to aim for objectives and even, at times, to reach them, rather than seek ways of cutting already depleted budgets. Earners themselves can take control over their lives and do not live in fear of the awful scourges of employment and emigration. These represent tremendous advances in Irish society and no account of a changing Irish psyche can overlook the impact of the economic revolution. Chapter 3 is thus devoted to a brief account of the reasons for and nature of Irish economic growth.

The problem for the observer trying to make sense of change in a society is that so many factors can alter all at once and it is difficult to discern which factors are causally related and which are merely coterminous. Does economic progress, for example, imply a decline in formal religious observance or is the latter in fact a function of modernity? Does the decline of the extended family have economic or ideological roots (or both)? These types of questions are very difficult, at times impossible, to answer. However, the use of theories and models makes it easier to evaluate a whole series of complex social changes at once. In Chapter 4, two models, relevant to change in Ireland, are introduced, one dealing with the social-psychological consequences of economic change and the other examining aspects of the modernising process. These models in turn provide the mechanisms by which the many differences between Ireland today and in the past can be assessed.

One hugely important but non-economic difference between Ireland and other developed countries is its high levels of religiosity and the absence of anti-clericalism from the political spectrum. However, this unique marker in Western Europe may be disappearing; the decline of mass-going and church authority and significance will be assessed in Chapter 5.

An essential research resource, used first in Chapter 5, and relied upon throughout the remainder of the book, is material gathered by survey. The Eurobarometer survey series (large samples surveyed twice yearly in all countries in the EEC/EC/EU since 1970 on a variety of topics) as well as the ISSP data series (based on a broader set of countries than in the Eurobarometer but run over a shorter time span) will be used most commonly in later chapters.

The advantage of these ongoing professional large-scale surveys is that they allow the observer to track change over time as well as making comparisons across different societies. It must be remembered that, like opinion polls, they depend on sampling to generate estimates of the attitudes or reported behaviour of the general population. Thus, they provide inexact indicators that can never match the precision of, say, the census (where the aim is to survey every single member of the population). Nevertheless, by carefully selecting and assessing representative groups among the public, they permit inferences to be drawn about the wider society. Thus they are invaluable, though sadly and inexplicably underused by Irish researchers.

Religion's strange bedfellow, sex, is the main topic of Chapter 6. The regulation and control of sexuality have been a traditional part of the church's missionary position, as it were, and alternatives to the monogamous heterosexual nuclear family can be anticipated to increase in acceptability at least partly as a function of diminished church power. At the same time, those alternatives may become more attractive for people who live increasingly individualistic and unfettered lifestyles.

Chapter 7 examines the character of Irish political life both in the narrow or conventional sense as well as in its broader nature (public opinion about it, popular interest in it, "alternative" political expression, racism, the environment, etc.). The potential diversity of political discourse is captured by data-gathering of a broad nature — on routine expressions of political taste, such as elections, general opinion poll and survey data as well as extraordinary events such as tribunals and crises. Chapters 8 and 9 progress naturally from this discussion but are in tension with one another, since the former examines the responsibilities of the state and state funding over time while the latter looks at individual consumer patterns and the consumption explosion in recent years. Chapters 8 and 9 thus provide some conclusions about the winner in the tussle over public versus private consumption. This conflict is at the core of the final discussion chapter.

Chapters 10 and 11 break up the Irish population along three important dimensions — gender, age and income grouping — in order to assess differential change. The ambition of the book therefore is to be comparative at three different levels. To compare the current Ireland with that of the past is the most important goal. A second comparative goal is to assess Ireland's performance or status with those of our international neighbours, especially in the EU. And finally, the fate of men versus women, rich versus poor and old versus young is examined to see whether change in Ireland has occurred evenly or in a preferential manner.[1]

In the final chapter, an overall assessment of the new Irish psyche is offered. The question posed is whether the recent boom has made us more materialistic and driven by financial considerations (the Thatcherite experience all over again); or alternatively, whether the years of financial success have permitted us to become less materialistic — that the partial resolution of material concerns means we can worry about other, "higher" concerns. Should or can we be proud of the last number of years? Have we much to show for our success? What, in essence, is the balance sheet on the changes in Irish society? How profound have they been and how should they be interpreted? This book is written with these questions in mind.

---

[1] When "Ireland" and "Irish" are used throughout the text, the reference is to the Republic of Ireland. This simply serves both as convenient shorthand and in recognising that the dynamics of social change north and south, although interlinked, are quite different.

Chapter Two

THE OLD IRISH PSYCHE

Memory Lane

One of the problems of comprehensive social change is the simple difficulty of remembering just how things were before. When a venerable aged citizen tells you that you honestly can't imagine how it was in the old days, it is not necessarily a case of misplaced nostalgia. It really is hard to recapture a place, to imagine meadows where there are now houses or winding country lanes in the place of four-lane motorways. And if this is true of physical environments, then it is all the harder to recall atmosphere or the sense and feel of another time. At least photographs fix the physical dimensions of the past. There are no counterparts for ambience although sometimes the music of an era (or, even more whimsically, a smell or taste) may bring the mood of another time to overwhelm one's thoughts in a Proustian rush.

I graduated from university in the late 1980s and like most of the students in my class emigrated immediately. I returned to live in Ireland only four years later but within that four years a qualitative shift in public attitudes had without doubt taken place and in fact was accelerating further. When I left, divorce was unavailable and homosexual acts were criminalised. I also seem to recall that advertisements for tampons were not permitted on RTE while machines in pubs may have sold cigarettes or shaving packs, but certainly not condoms (the sight of them in pub toilets in Holyhead always generated a *frisson* of adolescent excitement). On return to Ireland, I found that a divorce referendum which proved to be successful (only just) was looming, homosexuality had been decriminalised, we had learned to cope with references to menstruation on TV and were sophisticated enough to buy rubber sheaths when we chose to. Those were not inconsequential liberties in themselves but it can be argued that even more important was the change in values that they reflected. For what was really dramatic was that the mood of the people had shifted. The whole public discourse was different and a pervasive sense of oppression and control had been lifted. It didn't usher in a complete era of liberation by any means but certainly one felt a lot freer than previously.

The problem, though, as I say, is memory and when new freedoms are introduced the difficulty is recalling how things were in the past, how claustrophobic the atmosphere. Any *aides-memoires* to the emotions of the past are impressionistic and lack the clarity of, say, a photograph with its clear physical representation. Television clips from the 1970s showing men with big sideburns and some oddly tailored suits may but help only a little. Since one vital component of any widespread belief or ideology is permanence — that is, as things are now, they shall be for ever and ever amen — then inevitably hindsight and attempts to understand the past are at best distorted and at worst made impossible by the knowledge that things *did* change. What was once the all-important "now" is now only a historical curiosity. But since the aim here is to present an analysis of the New Irish Psyche, I am obliged to try to make sense of where we've come from, what we were. We cannot fully appreciate the New Irish Psyche without first remembering the Old Irish Psyche.

A Historian Writes

The skill of historians is the ability to place themselves in a point within the past, with all the prejudices and fears, loves, hates and stupidities of the time. The untrained historian falls prey to what has been called the Whig Fallacy of History — the assumption that all events in the past lead logically and directly to the present. Joseph Lee's (1989) history of Ireland in the twentieth century contains no such fallacies and is rightly celebrated for its scholarship, perspective and unyielding, even brutal, honesty about the nature of the Irish people and their society. He concludes the book with an extended chapter, which could have been published as a short book in its own right, called "Perspectives" in which he ventures some ideas about the Irish character, psyche and identity. (How pleasant to see a historian interested in psychological phenomena!) The emerging picture of Irishness is a grim one, stained with envy and bitterness.

Lee argues that since southern Ireland emerged under the shadow of her imperialist master relatively recently, the attitudes of the people were inevitably and thoroughly marked by this event. Lee argues that "the dependency syndrome . . . had wormed its way into the Irish psyche during the long centuries of foreign dominance. The Irish mind was enveloped in, and to some extent suffocated by, an English mental embrace" (p. 627). Irish people were familiar, as a servant to his master, with England, but really only with England, and not with other countries. On independence, there was a "seductive" appeal of using English ideas, legal systems, models and intellectual solutions to Irish problems. The difficulty of course was that Ireland was a country on a very different scale, qualitatively and quantitatively, to England and faced distinctive challenges that required novel and unique solutions. As Lee puts it, "absorption in the English model gravely limited Irish perspectives. When allied to the elusive but crucial psychological factors that inspired the instinct of inferiority, it shrivelled Irish perspectives on Irish potential" (p. 629). For much of the twentieth century, there was a failure to develop an intellectual independence to match the new political autonomy.

Appropriate models for our development were available. These were not the decaying, still vast and mighty empires, but rather small European countries, some on the periphery of Europe. Many of them had suffered both at the hands of external larger forces as well as the effects of civil war (one or two were even languishing after their own grandiose attempts to build empires). Yet countries like Norway, Denmark, Sweden, Finland, Switzerland, the Netherlands and Belgium performed at stunning levels in many ways. This was not simply in the basic (but essential) goal of being able to sustain ever-growing populations in good health and without the threat of mass unemployment, but also outside the realm of economics as each country made profound contributions to an international intellectual life within areas as diverse as the natural sciences, sociology, demographics, and economic theory. As Lee says (p. 603):

> At any given population level, and at any level of income per head, other small northern European countries, without exception, appear to have devoted significantly more resources [than Ireland] to the effort to understand society in general and their own society in particular.

They also succeeded in many cases in being able to sustain and advance the use of their national language while also respecting the advantages, cultural and economic, that would accrue by educating their citizens to use other languages fluently. They became, in different ways and to varying degrees, models of success and their psychology was one mainly of self-confidence and self-belief.

In contrast, Lee suggests that the Irish developed a far-from-noble outlook which was at once a blend of self-pity, a hostility to all things English and a slavish imitation of the former colonial master. Hypocrisy, while not uniquely Irish, was one of the few things at which we excelled. Clear informed thinking, the synthesis of ideas into something original, and the ethic of hard work were replaced by rote and formula, the fragmentation of decision-making into a meaninglessly small division of labour (reflected in the modus operandi of the Irish civil service) and torpor. This torpor or inactivity was reflected, as well as created, by an academic generation for whom research work was less a chore than a source of moral degradation. Lee provides a delicious example from the 1930s of a member of a medical faculty in UCG being condemned, through a unanimous vote, by his colleagues. His crime? "Guilty of the indiscretion of research work" (p. 617). Lee suggests that even the description of Irish culture as anti-intellectual

> . . . may be too generous. [It] may be more sub-intellectual than anti-intellectual. Anti-intellectualism is too intellectually demanding. (p. 577)

The sloth that characterised thinking among academics was also common to journalists, government advisers and Catholic Church "thinkers". And it had a mirror image in Ireland's sluggish patterns of production. Within agriculture and industry, there was a reliance on the old and short-term easy ways and a failure to comprehend that a small country must rely on innovation and flexibility. The direct consequence was a shoddy economic performance as well as its two handmaidens — emigration and stagnation. As was noted in Chapter 1, the experience and fear of emigration are deeply etched into the Irish psyche. This is a widely known and hardly cutting-edge revelation. Lee's analysis is more far-reaching, though: because emigration was so numerically and emotionally devastating in real and relative proportions for Ireland, the whole society was shaped to deal with the phenomenon. Emigration was in fact an essential safety valve for social peace (since such a sluggish and stagnant economy could not deal with hundreds of thousands of people demanding a reasonable living) and served therefore, the interests of the possessor class in general and large farmers in particular. Ideologies were required in order to explain how a simple, warm, Catholic and homogeneous society continued to survive only by expelling sizeable chunks of its numbers on an annual basis. While a crude Brit-blaming nationalism was often drawn upon, it suffered serious credibility deficits by the 1950s. Organised religion and the media too played a valuable role in normalising the socio-pathological patterns of emigration. When all else failed, the victim would suffice — "Irish emigration was, to an extent unusual in Europe, female emigration" (Lee, 1985: 376). Many Irish women preferred to take their chances elsewhere rather than staying and choosing between unemployment, the convents or the "ballroom of romance" that was rural Ireland:

> . . . far from the society bearing responsibility, the fickleness of
> the female personality now sufficed to explain an otherwise
> baffling indictment of an axiomatically innocent society, basking
> contentedly in its own smug sense of moral superiority. (p. 376)

Is this not reminiscent of good ole Southern boys in the pre-civil rights US, blaming social unrest on uppity blacks?

The sexual world of Old Ireland was far from healthy. Stagnancy produces an obsession with inheritance — thus there was a corresponding obsession with morality, or sexual morality, to be more precise. Lee argues that the message of the Catholic church around the gift of celibacy (about the gift of sexuality the church was far less eager to preach) was to reconcile those who endured the long wait before marriage and discourage inheritance-threatening "accidents". It was no accident therefore that the church was obsessed with sexual morality rather than any other kind, such as the (im)morality of inequality, sexism, violence, or hypocrisy. And just as there are good material reasons why the sexual world of the time was perverse, in the real sense of the world, the personality or character of an individual trying to survive such an environment was typically marked.

We use the term "begrudgery" quite frequently to refer to the way in which Irish people often resent the success of others. But perhaps the term is too quaint or too gentle — a "meanness of spirit" may be more descriptive. That the environment should generate this meanness — this envy, this septic isle — is perfectly logical. A sluggish society that cannot learn or grow is condemned merely to survive. And in a stagnant economy, what is good for you is bad for me, since the size of the cake is fixed. Thus, one's man gain is another's loss. Therefore every success by another citizen of the state represents a theft of that which might be mine or that of my children (the non-emigrating ones at any rate). And thus the pattern of spite, of envy, of malice and gossip, of ridiculing the success or even survival of others, of thwarted ambition is our legacy today.

Lee has presented a vision of the past which is bleak; a slothful, aping, barren society, sexually repressed, hypocritical, embittered and cruel, yet unbearably smug and conceited at the same time.

A More Sympathetic Analysis

Geraldine Moane (1994), like Lee, has recognised the impact that colonisation had on the Irish people and continued to do so, through the process of decolonisation, for generations. Her account is a good deal more sympathetic than Lee's and she draws heavily on Franz Fanon's (1968) anti-imperialist analysis as well as feminist concepts of patriarchal oppression. She suggests that psyche and society are "intrinsically interconnected" and that therefore any attempts to describe the "Irish character" or "Irish psyche" risk being static and monolithic;

in other words, if society changes, then presumably the national "character" also changes. (I agree, incidentally — hence this book.)

Moane argues that Ireland experienced, in its own distinctive way, all the effects of colonisation — specifically:

> . . . a history of military invasion and defeat, dispossession and appropriation of economic wealth, exclusion to varying degrees from political power, attempted erasure of language and culture, production of an ideology by the colonisers which regarded "the natives" as inferior, a litany of failed attempts at resistance, betrayal and collusion. (p. 253)

These processes began in Ireland much earlier than the "age of imperialism", Europe's vast programme of colonisation, especially of Africa. The psychological implications of colonisation thus shaped the Irish psyche, she suggests. Moane argues that a primary theme of the colonised mind is fear, from the violence exerted by the coloniser. A second theme common in the literature of colonisation is ambivalence towards, and even dependency on, the coloniser. The feeling of ambivalence requires a suppression of anger and rage. A sense of inferiority and a loss of identity also usually accompany the process. Overall, colonisation can be seen to brutalise both coloniser and colonised. For the colonised, this leads to difficulties with sexual identity, horizontal violence (directing anger at peers rather than "superiors") as well as vulnerability to psychological distress.

The post-colonial personality struggles to free itself at the psychological level just as mass movements have done at a political one. Moane follows Kenny (1985) to argue that the continuing ambivalence towards the coloniser produce both personal and social withdrawal. Social withdrawal is expressed through superficial compliance and poor and indirect communication and can result in "passive aggression, evasiveness, understatement, backbiting and avoidance of competition" (p. 259). Personal withdrawal involves "helplessness, passivity and elaboration of the inner self" (p. 259). Other typical post-colonial features are a lack of pride, divisiveness between Irish people, a narrow identity of the meaning of Irishness, a lack of assertiveness and a tendency to oppress others. Moane suggests that the evasiveness and indirectness of communication of the Irish have been remarked on by outsiders when visiting Ireland, and begrudgery can be seen as a form of horizontal hostility. Overall, while Moane's account is sympathetic, the damaged nature of the colonised and post-colonial personality is nonetheless implicit.

Irish Catholic History as Irish History

The authority of the Catholic church as a source of ideological power has been mentioned but perhaps not stressed enough. And indeed it is difficult to overrate the importance of the church in deciphering the Old Irish Psyche since, for most of the twentieth century, being Irish meant being Irish Catholic — the history of Irishness is quite often the history of Irish Catholicism. National and religious identities were interwoven, generating an ideological exclusion of Protestants and other religious minorities. (More a Catholic than a catholic society, one might argue.) The sociologist Tom Inglis has offered a sophisticated account for the way in which church hegemony was exercised. The title of his book is *Moral Monopoly: The Rise and Fall of the Catholic Church in Modern Ireland*. This edition was published in 1998 — the first edition was published in 1987 and the then subheading was "The Catholic Church in Modern Irish Society". The title change and its timing are not incidental — one at the beginning and the other near the end of the economic boom. But the core of the title in both editions, "Moral Monopoly", is well-chosen since it captures something of the power of the church — for so long not merely a player but *the* player in the Irish moral sphere, the supreme arbiter on right and wrong in this country.

Steven Lukes, in his short but persuasive book on the nature of power (1974), has argued that it is most effective when it is exercised in a situation where those who are complying believe it to be in their best interests to do so. Catholic influence in Ireland has had that complete and penetrating character — all (or most) felt ownership over it, it was perceived as the simple, deep and devout faith of the people. And from this arose its influence over every area of life. Inglis commences his book with some insightful reminiscences into his own childhood — how his mother attended mass every day, how Catholic rituals, large and small, were part of his life. He points out that "we did not talk much about religion; we practised it" (p. 1). Thus apart from mass on Sunday, he remembers abstaining from meat on Friday, giving up sweets during Lent, saying the rosary as well as taking part in May and October devotions. Alongside the bliss of setting up a shrine to Our Lady in his bedroom (although in this, one has to say, he was an especially devout child), he remembers the fear of hell and his awe of priests.

The Catholic church was fundamental in structuring how Irish people lived, how they related to one another and how they viewed the world. It made decisions as practical as to who got certain jobs; it managed schools, hospitals and churches; it provided definitions of what it meant to be a "decent" person as well as parameters within which government policy should (and did) operate. It hovered at birth and death. It made policy on culture, which went way beyond merely commenting on the acceptability of the arts and literature at the time. If it is to be protested that it was "we", not "it" (the church) who were responsible, since we were of the church, then the point is missed and the nature of church power is underestimated. It was the overwhelming hold of the church as a mobilising force that made Irish life unique. Where else in Europe in the second half of the twentieth century could a bishop provoke a national debate by criticising a woman who may have not worn a nightdress on her wedding night?

And this is the nature of its monopoly — control over every part of life, including (and especially) those deemed the most intimate or private. But things have clearly changed (see Chapters 5 and 6 for further evidence of this) and the Old Irish Psyche has virtually disappeared. To whom or what does a monopoly lose its power? Inglis' argument is instructive in this regard. He suggests that the strength of the church lay in a strategic alliance with certain sections of Irish society. However, this was also its Achilles heel, since without that alliance, it could not exert the same overwhelming totalitarian (in both its older, literal, as well as modern, pejorative sense) control. The most important coalition formed by the Catholic church was with Irish mothers, argues Inglis. Although Irish women have been largely omitted from Irish history,

> . . . the crucial role of the mother in passing on the Catholic
> faith from one generation to the next and instilling a devotion
> and loyalty to the institutional church is only beginning to be
> recognised (Inglis, 1998: 178).

The famine and other related factors in the mid-nineteenth century
broke the economic power of Irish women outside the home, since
they ushered in less labour-intensive livestock farming (as opposed
to tillage farming) where women's labour was less valued, saw the
replacement of domestic weaving industry by steam-driven machines
in Britain and the decline in the proportion of small farmers to large
(women enjoyed more equality with the former) (see Crotty, 1966;
Lee, 1989). The church formed an alliance with the large tenant
farmer, but more especially with his wife:

> It was the mother who became the organisational link be-
> tween the newly institutionalised power of the Roman Catho-
> lic Church and the individual farming family. It was she who in-
> stilled and maintained in her husband and children all that was
> disciplined, moral and civil. (Inglis, 1998: 184)

The church recognised and used the power of mothers over the
domestic sphere to maintain their wider social hegemony. The
training of girls was stressed by the religious in schools, not just in
household care but as good mothers. Priests and nuns gained control of the sexual life of women by portraying them as weak and vulnerable to sinful temptations. They had to be protected not from but
through ignorance — "outside the confessional there was a deafen-
ing silence. Sex became the most abhorrent sin" (p. 188). The puri-
tan sexual morality was first instilled into Irish mothers by clergy and
then mothers were expected to reproduce this morality among their
daughters. Ritual practices like the rosary were the occasion when
the mother exercised her moral power over the family. Pleasure
came from these devotions, especially to Our Lady. On the other
hand, sex was something repulsive, to be endured, not enjoyed.

Fathers, on the other hand, were socialised to believe that expression of much interest in their children was a sign at least of im-
maturity, if not femininity. The emotional management of the family
was left to a mother who did not consider using her talents outside

the home (since that would destroy family life and give bad example to daughters — as Pope Pius XII claimed). She had to decide which son would get the farm, which would apply for priesthood and which should be readied to accept emigration. Daughters were reared to be good mothers, or chaste for the convent or prepared for emigration. Children who tried to buck the roles set out for them were "slagged" and cut down to size by the ridicule of their mothers, siblings and peers.

Is the Past Another Country?

The more one remembers an older Ireland and reads accounts of an even older one, the more difficult it is to like the society or feel much beyond pity for its citizens. Undoubtedly there were good points, and certainly many visitors to this society from elsewhere appeared to like it. But then they could go back home and get away from it again. In the same way, Irish women today can enjoy holidays in certain conservative Islamic countries *despite* certain aspects of their culture, but would certainly be reluctant to live there. And the sense of entrapment and smothering claustrophobia is one that has lingered until very recently.

Tim Pat Coogan, editor of *The Irish Press* from the late 1960s to the late 1980s, and both insider and outside politically, also tried to capture the era in his book, *Disillusioned Decades: Ireland 1966–87*. The title of his book is instructive, even if his analysis is less so. But simply seeing again the headlines and debates of the time brings a little shudder of remembrance. Anne Lovett, a teenager dying alone during childbirth in a field in Granard in 1984, even though her pregnancy had been noted and spoken about (and ignored) by some adults. A second earlier case, in 1983, involved the sacking of a secondary school teacher, Eileen Flynn, by a religious order because she was living with and became pregnant by a married man whose wife had left him. The court, as well as most of the Irish public, agreed with the sacking — she was giving the local youth a bad example. And, of course, in 1985, the tribunal into the decision of the Gardai to prosecute Joanne Hayes for the murder of an infant in Cahirciveen is most memorable.

> [There was a] . . . feeling that for a time a veil had been lifted
> on a primitive and rather terrifying Ireland that was probably
> more widespread than the good churchgoers of the country
> liked to imagine. (Coogan, 1987: 80)

And alongside the sexual morality plays of the time, Coogan recalls, in this pre-Tiger era, the "brash young men in the mohair suits" of Fianna Fáil — and how "nobody questioned their corner-cutting and wheeler-dealing" (p. 1). At least now we call it corruption. The society was not merely characterised by trademark problems of under-developed societies like this. Coogan recalls how very modern diffi-culties also emerged — a heroin scourge in Dublin, and a corre-sponding crime problem, both of which were exacerbated by the poor planning and hyper-urbanisation of the inner city as well as the new satellite developments of Tallaght, Ballymun and Clondalkin (their torments must be at least partly blamed on the sleazy repre-sentatives and officials who put brown envelopes ahead of thoughtful urban designing).

Aside from Tom Inglis, what have Irish sociologists generally had to say about the evolution of this society? Or indeed, how have they interpreted the Irish mind? To be fair, sociologists have rarely claimed to be studying the national "mind", indulging themselves with only occasional forays into "ideology" instead. But their contribution is still limited by certain factors. Psychologists of international repute like Jerome Bruner have suggested that the discipline of psychology "seems to have lost its centre and its great integrating questions" (quoted in Benson, 2001: ix) but the specialisation and absence of synthesis is even truer of sociology, especially in an Irish context. One of the exceptions can be found in the work of Luke Gibbons (1996) who has tried to escape from the "edited volume" book for-mat (a useful way of gathering distinct positions on an issue but inevi-tably tending towards a disjointed narrative) in his writings on Irish culture. Of most relevance to this chapter is Gibbons' essay on the myth of modernisation in Ireland. He proposes that it was in the early 1980s that a novel belief was ushered in — the belief that a new Ireland had appeared (the same view has gained currency again, of course). The signs then may have been just as powerful — on the left, there was a feeling that increased urbanisation and industrialisation had neutralised nationalism as a political force. The IDA made much of the fact that more than half of the population was under the age of 25 (and those nauseating Young European ads were everywhere — see Chapter 11). Gibbons suggests that the broadcasting of *The Ballroom of Romance* in 1982 was particularly symbolic. Since its central theme was the Old Ireland of the 1950s with all its sexual repression, poverty, emigration, it appeared to offer reassurance that modern Ireland was definitely with us — and *Ballroom* was offering a view on our tragic past. The reality of the 1980s though, argues Gibbons, was chronic unemployment, the reappearance of mass emigration, the Granard and Kerry Babies tragedies/controversies, a new censorship mentality as well as moving statues (in Ballinspittle in 1984 and sporadically in every second village for the following year) as well as the resurgence of unreconstructed nationalism during the hunger strikes in 1981.

> If a Rip Van Winkle fell asleep in the 1950s and woke up in 1988, he could be forgiven for thinking that nothing had changed in between. Even the Brylcreem look and baggy trousers were back in vogue . . . (Gibbons, 1996: 83)

Gibbons provides a warning to those writing analyses of change. What Ireland was and what it has become is not as self-evident as we might like to think (just as foot-and-mouth disease, representing, at the time of writing, an ongoing crisis in the UK and a continuing concern for Ireland, is not what we expected of 2001 — it's just *so* 1967). In particular, mythical notions of Old Ireland, exaggerations of the distinctiveness of the present and a refusal to recognise continuities with the past must undermine any attempt to assess modernity and post-modernity in this society. Those who make claims of change must provide both evidence and explanations for the phenomenon. In their absence, elaborate and earnest but ultimately worthless social models are built on foundations of sand.

Notwithstanding Gibbons' claim, the belief of this author is that a qualitative change has occurred of fundamental importance in Irish society in recent times and by implication in the character or psyche of its members. Elements of this change might be reversible and further change should also be anticipated, but it surely must be conceded that it is impossible to talk about Ireland in the same way as before. Economic, political, religious and sexual norms have shifted in ways that make meaningful the phrase "the past is another country". Gibbons' essay, though, is a nice illustration of the threats of impressionism, hazy thinking and simple lapses of memory. These errors may be forgivable in the case of the public, understandable for journalists and inevitable for politicians, but for the serious social scientist, memory and perception are not enough. The available evidence must be examined, and in as fair-minded a way as possible. Claims of change must be supported with clear and unambiguous data from reliable sources, rather than accepted opinion.

However, as was made clear in the first chapter, the aim of this book is not only to trace the rapid evolution of this society based on solid indicators but also to offer an assessment of its merits. From the sketches given above of the way we used to be, one is tempted to say that almost any change must be good. Regardless of perspective — historical, sociological and social psychological — the image of old Ireland is a grim one. While one may attempt to put a positive spin on the reasons for that, there is a fair deal of consensus that this was a bleak, economically feeble, intellectually closed, begrudging, priest-ridden, sexually repressed but also hypocritical and smug land. And since it couldn't have got a lot worse, then things, as the song goes, could only get better. Does that seem unfair? Was there maybe a closeness of community or a neighbourliness, even a kindness, as well as a naivete or innocence, that have been lost? Perhaps, but few seem to have noted it then or to miss it now. And it's hard to square kindness with paedophile priests, corrupt politicians and routine mass emigration (although they certainly required the preconditions of naivete and innocence). And maybe the worst legacy of the past was the way it shaped the future. Perhaps given its awfulness, we have been racing from what we were towards what we are now without much reflection or planning in between — a change based on panic and self-disgust. This theme is taken up in the final chapter.

Chapter Three

NOUVEAU RICHE: DISSECTING THE NEW ECONOMIC REALITY

What's in a Name?

It's a general rule that the initial catchiness of a phrase is directly proportional to its subsequent odiousness. Most likely it's to do with
Ireland's small population, but normally phrases that are lightly caned
elsewhere are flogged to death here. As a nation, we have a great ear
for the hackneyed. If I were given a pound for every time I've heard
or read "Celtic Tiger", I would be a rich but still irritated man.
"Celtic Tiger" has become a national mantra, used in praise but inevitably also in anger (e.g. the juxtaposition of some pressing social
problem with — or more usually, *despite* — the Celtic Tiger). It's
universally heard, liberally used and terribly annoying. Lazy journalists
probably mutter it in their sleep. The problem though, and here's the
catch, is that "Celtic Tiger" is perfectly apt for the Irish economy.

The tiger economies, of course, originally referred to the Asian
Tigers, especially South Korea, Singapore, Hong Kong and Taiwan.
Their spectacular double-digit annual growth from the early 1970s
onwards provided hope to a shaky international capitalist system,
reeling as it was from the oil crisis and the imperialist adventures of
the US in south-east Asia. It's quite a compliment, one might imagine,
to join this group of energetic overachievers. However, it should be
remembered that they had something in common apart from their
rapid growth, something a little less flattering on reflection. They are
used as examples of countries in the *developing* world that achieved

economic success *despite* the backwardness of their economies in the late 1960s. In other words, what distinguishes them is not only their rapid rate of improvement but their appallingly low starting points. As even Stalin's Russia made clear, spectacular economic progress is possible (although certainly not inevitable) when the jumping-off point is a condition of utter poverty. And these societies could register phenomenal improvements in their industrial production only because they had started with virtually none.

In Ireland, we were delighted to be associated with these moderately successful quasi-police states (although one wouldn't like to be in their economic shoes right now). Our growth rate in Europe was spectacular in the 1990s, not because we were racing ahead of our neighbours, but because we were racing to catch up. It is worthwhile reflecting on the 1950s and 1960s, the so-called "Golden Age of Capitalism". The genius of Irish post-independence political leadership was such that as a well-positioned English-speaking country with a great deal of natural resources surrounded by a rapidly growing world economy, Ireland managed to stagnate, even wither. Some of these geniuses should be asked to explain how we ended up being flattered by comparison to countries whose success occurred despite the very different and far more substantial difficulties they faced. And this was towards the end of a century in which most of our closest European neighbours had long since shot ahead and were basking in the economic equivalent of their autumnal years.

From Basket Case to Shining Light

But this is churlish. No doubt Ireland too had its demons and managed with time to overcome them. If we did, like our Asian cousins, start our development late and modestly, nonetheless our recent growth rates have been, well, tigerish, for lack of a better word. The main purpose in this chapter is to highlight just how great were the economic changes experienced in Ireland in the last decade or so. This is important in the context of the book, since fundamental changes in a nation's material living conditions will impact upon its psyche, outlook, and confidence. Sometimes it is argued that geography makes people who they are — the island home of the British, it has been suggested, made them eccentric and suspicious of foreigners. Greek philosophers believed that Asians lacked aggression because of their cool weather and frequent rainfall (relative to Greece, presumably!). We often think of Mediterraneans as carefree and warm. However, by and large, geographical or meteorological determinism gets short shrift these days. But economic determinism is widely accepted — few people doubt that money maketh the man (and woman). And as explained in Chapter 1, the aim of this book is to try to assess the degree and manner in which economic change in Ireland has, along with other forces, changed the people living here. Two broad models seeking to describe the interaction between growth and psychological change at a societal scale are outlined in greater detail in the next chapter — while this chapter is devoted to an analysis of the recent economic boom, its magnitude and origins.

It is well known that people make sense of events in their environment not in an even-handed way but in a biased one, usually with spectacular self-aggrandisement or defence, depending upon circumstance. Thus, empirical studies confirm that politicians attribute domestic success to their own policies and failure to broader world trends. With delightful predictability, *The Making of the Celtic Tiger: The Inside Story of Ireland's Economic Boom* appeared in late 2000 and was co-written by Ray MacSharry, Minister of Finance from 1987–88, and Padraig White, managing director of the IDA from 1981–90. This attempt, one of many, to claim paternity over the Celtic Tiger contrasts sharply with the poor bastard child of early 1980s recession, about which no political insider accounts were written. To be fair to MacSharry and White, the book does present a thoroughgoing account of the economic changes during the boom, despite its self-congratulatory nature. Furthermore, a good deal of credit is given to Alan Dukes and the Tallaght strategy speech in 1987 (in which Fine Gael support for a fiscally prudent minority Fianna Fáil government was guaranteed).

MacSharry and White cite Joseph Lee's comment that "Irish economic performance has been the least impressive in Western Europe, perhaps in all Europe, in the twentieth century" (2000: 40). However the eminent historian had made the comment in his book,

Ireland 1912–1985: Politics and Society, a book that appeared in the late 1980s and which has been discussed at length in Chapter 2. His book concluded at a particularly low point in Irish economic fortunes and must have influenced his outlook. And the early to mid-1980s were a grim time here by any set of indices. The growth rate, sluggish in the late 1970s, was especially poor in the early to mid-1980s and GNP actually fell in 1982, 1983 and 1986. MacSharry and White also contend that fiscal policy had become increasingly reckless during the oil crisis and subsequent fuel-price hikes as governments breached an unwritten rule that borrowing should not be used for day-to-day government expenditure (borrowing for capital spending was justified in that such debt at least generated fixed assets). The national debt rose alarmingly, with spiralling interest, so that in 1986 it stood at 129 per cent of GNP (it had been below 70 per cent of GNP only a decade and a half earlier). Servicing of the public debt alone consumed 93.5 per cent of income tax revenue. High interest rates prevailing at the time made owing money all the more expensive.

Ireland joined the Exchange Rate Mechanism (ERM) in 1979 but continued to track sterling for a number of years, rather than the low inflation deutschmark. Ireland's annual inflation rate in 1981 was nearly 20.5 per cent but was gradually reduced to just over 3 per cent in 1987. Problematically, the low inflation rate was in part a consequence of the high unemployment rate of the time since, by 1986, a record 226,000, or 17 per cent of the workforce, were jobless. And this shocking level actually flattered the number of work opportunities available at the time because of emigration levels. The flood of people leaving Ireland was probably the truest indication of the capacity of the economy. By the mid-1980s, emigration was no longer a safety valve; it was a massive indictment of economic failure. It was experienced across class-lines, except that working class kids left the country when they were 17 or 18 while the middle-classes enjoyed their state-subsidised university education before leaving for slightly more comfortable jobs elsewhere. The gradual disappointments and stresses of living one's teenage years in a country patently unable to provide one with subsequent useful or indeed any employment are difficult to assess but cannot be underestimated. (Even in wartime, young people feel more valued by their state; see Galbraith's (1999) recollection that most Americans preferred the wartime years of the 1940s over the 1930s depression.)

But how the times have changed. The "basket case" economy, in 1986–87 with the "statistics of a third world country" (MacSharry, 2000: 356) has dragged itself into a leading position economically. In 1999, the OECD report on Ireland hailed "five straight years of stunning economic performance. No other OECD member country has been able to match its outstanding outcomes in a variety of dimensions." Helpfully, MacSharry and White include some tables providing summary information about some key dimensions of the economy. These tables tell the story of improvement in the last years of the 1990s. Our growth rate per annum in the 1990s has raced well ahead of the OECD average (about 2 per cent) at around 7 per cent for the entire decade or about 9 per cent for the last five years of the decade. The numbers employed in industry but especially the services sector have increased while those working in agriculture have declined, a classic sign of economic modernisation. The number of trade disputes from 1994–1998 was lower than at any time since before the 1960s. Deficit budgeting is definitely out of vogue and while in the 1980s, finance ministers were habitually plagued with problems of cost-cutting, in the last few years the problem of how to spend massive surpluses has exercised Minister McCreevy. Politically popular income tax reduction has been made possible on both the higher and lower income rates as well as through increases in the tax-free allowance. National debt as a proportion of GNP has been declining since it approached 130 per cent in 1986–87 to close to 60 per cent at the time of writing. The inflation rate was kept closely under control (until recently).

The boom has transformed peoples' lives. Economic growth has been real and not simply an accounting exercise on a balance sheet. Changes in employment levels are little short of amazing, with long-term unemployment at only about 2 per cent in 1999. In Figure 3.1 below, the monthly figures for the percentage of the labour force officially out of work is shown for the period January 1996 to April

2001. It presents a picture of almost linear decline. And this has not been achieved at the cost of further emigration or a declining workforce. The total number in employment has actually increased very rapidly, from 1,494,500 in March/May 1998 to 1,670,700 in March/May 2000, only two years later. And perhaps most psychologically satisfying of all, the numbers living in the country are increasing through natural population but also through migration. Yes, people actually want to move to Ireland and to live here again. While emigration has continued (and in 1995 it slightly exceeded immigration), net migration was modest but positive in the last four years of the decade, with a CSO estimate of 22,300 leaving the country in 2000 while 42,300 entered it to live here in the same year. (About half of all immigrants in 2000 were former Irish emigrants returning to live here while about another 30 per cent were split evenly between UK and EU citizens. The CSO estimates for 2001[1] suggested that returning Irish made up a slightly smaller proportion than in 2000 with immigrants from other than the EU and US increasing from about 8,000 to 12,000).

Figure 3.1: Seasonally Adjusted Monthly (Standardised) Unemployment Rates in Ireland, January 1996 to April 2001

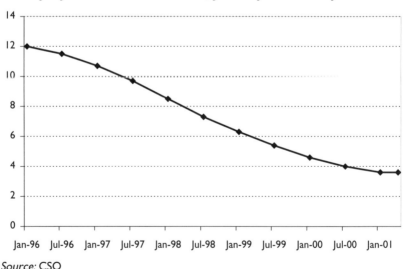

Source: CSO

---

[1] CSO News Release reference 184/2001

While more people are working, their wages are also rising with real take-home pay estimated by NESC (report no. 105) to have increased throughout the late 1980s and 1990s. The GNP of Ireland in 1973 was below 60 per cent of the average of the 15 current members of the EU. In 1999, it was recorded as 93 per cent of the EU average and climbing fast (and the EU includes the wealthiest regions in the world, like south-east England, eastern France and the Paris basin, Emilia-Romagna and much of northern Italy, southern Germany and so on). On budget day 2000, the Taoiseach announced that Ireland was now on a 100 per cent par with EU GNP. Most satisfying of all, no doubt, particularly for Fianna Fáilers, was that the figures contrived to show that Ireland's GDP had exceeded that of our colonial masters in Britain in the late 1990s. The context of this is important — Tansey (1998) has shown that, again with the EU states' average set at 100 per cent, Ireland's GDP from 1961 to 1970 was 60.5 per cent compared to the UK figure of 112.5 per cent.

Behind the Boom

What are the reasons for the boom? The most obvious, although least often stated, is the cyclical nature of economics and the manner in which very sharp recessions often lay the groundwork for equally sharp periods of growth (this truism is underplayed because the worrying corollary also holds — bust invariably follows boom). Recession makes people eager for work, creates a hunger for opportunity and focuses the mind clearly on priorities. The deep economic crisis of the early 1980s laid the mindset for growth as well as forcing hundreds of thousands to emigrate. Obvious to Ray MacSharry as a kickstart to progress was a capable political class who learned the lessons of fiscal prudence and stepped in before the IMF was forced to. The peace process in Northern Ireland probably improved the perception of the entire island of Ireland by other parts of the world but the impact is difficult to assess. Historically, the abolition of secondary school fees under Minister of Education Donogh O'Malley in 1966 was also important in creating a literate workforce capable of dealing with change (although see below for further discussion of the education issue).

Other events such as joining the EEC at the beginning of 1973 are also now recognised as crucial to development, in terms of tariff-free access to a vast market, an ideology of low inflation and, perhaps most crucially, through financial transfers from the EU CAP and Structural funds. Certainly Ireland has been a stony ground for Euro-sceptic ideas heretofore, although now that we are expected to become net contributors to the EU, and poorer countries are poised to join the Union, it will be interesting to assess the growth of Euro-scepticism here (see a brief assessment of the Nice Treaty vote in Chapter 7). Funds from foreign investment were also attracted, especially using low corporate taxation as an incentive. Non-EU firms, mainly US ones, favour Ireland because of IDA support as well as certain characteristics such as an English-speaking workforce. Ireland's attractions include a relatively low tax and deregulated economic foothold within the EU as well as a hitherto cheap, plentiful and reasonably well-educated workforce.

Financial shock therapy is argued to have been an important factor in controlling public finances and thereby the whole economy. Externally, the constraints imposed by the desire to sign up to the single currency provided a stimulus towards balanced budgets. Internally a concord emerged around fiscal stability from the late 1980s and the Tallaght speech signalled an agreement by centre and right-wing parties on the nature of government spending. Perhaps of greater importance was the consensus achieved beyond government with the "social partners". In a series of agreements (The Programme for National Recovery [1987/88–1990], The Programme for Economic Prosperity [1990/91–1993], The Programme for Competitiveness and Work [1993/94–1996], Partnership 2000 [1997–2000] and the most recent Programme for Prosperity and Fairness), the unions were brought on board, sometimes reluctantly, and pay restraint was traded for future tax cuts. This provided the industrial peace with which to attract foreign investment. Alongside all of these factors were undoubtedly good fortune and timing as well as a virtuous circle of growth and confidence once the economy emanated a positive purr.

The Education Factor

Among the strongest self-beliefs or self-conceits of the Irish is that we are a well-educated people and that this has been a positive factor in determining high levels of growth. Paul Tansey (1998) outlines the importance of educational influences and examines their impact on the economy in Ireland (the value given to education as an end in itself, rather than an economic prop, will be assessed in Chapter 8). Human capital is:

> . . . the stock of economically relevant knowledge, skills and learning embodied in a population. Investments in education, training and knowledge add to the national stock of human capital. (Tansey, 1998: 98)

High quality labour (that is, appropriately and well-educated workers from the perspective of the employers) is more flexible and adaptive and can facilitate the introduction of new technologies. Tansey cites an interesting study by de la Fuente and Vives (1997), economists studying the growth rate of Spain, Portugal and Ireland. Their analysis suggested that although the three countries benefited from convergence effects (the tendency of lagging countries to catch up with industrial leaders because of the diffusion of technology), enhanced investments in human capital, such as education and training, were of great significance especially for Ireland. They contend that almost one-eighth of Ireland's above-average growth was a consequence of improved human capital.

Tansey argues that Ireland experienced an education revolution in the last 30 years. In that time, student numbers in secondary level trebled while numbers at third-level increased six-fold. In 1994, more than 80 per cent of Irish 17-year-olds were still at school compared to less than a quarter 30 years previously. Public spending reflects the greater priority given to education — as Tansey notes,

> . . . government spending on education increased from 3.1 per cent of GNP in 1961 to 6.5 per cent in 1993 . . . [and] against a background where real Gross Domestic Product itself has increased more than threefold. Hence, over the past three

decades, spending on Irish education has been taking larger
slices of a much bigger cake. (p. 117)

However, there are some worrying defects in the education system.
Satisfactory levels of literacy and numeracy are not obtained by all
and international surveys have placed Irish teenagers below average
in reading skills in comparison to other developed countries (reported in *The Sunday Tribune*, 1997, 31 August). The Government
White Paper on Education (1995) admitted that Irish 13-year-olds
have very low achievements in science compared to the same age
group in other countries. There is no nationwide standard examination in reading, writing and basic computation until most pupils are
about 15 years old (the Junior Certificate). About a quarter of young
Irish people leave school with no more than the basic compulsory
education and this in itself is a highly significant predictor of unemployment. Vocational and practical skills are poorly taught in Irish
secondary schools.

In the context of training in the workplace, O'Connell and Lyons
(1995) found little evidence of improvements in the low levels of
workplace training offered in Ireland. Other studies noted that Irish
expenditure on management training is poor by international standards. A NESC report (no. 95) accepted that Irish shopfloor workers have fewer formal qualifications than their EU counterparts and
the skills of supervisory staff are lower on average than elsewhere in
Europe.

Boom Sceptics

The concluding comments above are useful in introducing scepticism
about the economic boom, its achievements and origins. The difficulty, as Anthony Sweeney has pointed out (see below), is that one
of the first casualties of an economic upturn is the belief that we can
ever be poor again. The problem for the social analyst in trying to
assess the effects of sudden growth is that one must be reasonably
confident that the growth is real, not a statistical illusion. At least a
majority of the population must enjoy and feel the fruit-of-the-boom
— otherwise, one can hardly anticipate a "new psyche". And some

sceptics have challenged the prevailing consensus, that the rising tide has lifted all yachts.

An important qualification about levels of growth here has been raised in Jonathan Haughton's (1998) interesting essay, "The Dynamics of Economic Change". One of his concerns is over the seemingly trivial difference between GDP and GNP. The Gross Domestic Product (GDP) of a country is a measure of the total output produced within the boundaries of the country "but in recent years this overstates the increase in incomes accruing to residents of [Ireland]" (p. 29). The Gross National Product (GNP) is the amount attributable to Irish workers and companies. GDP has outgrown GNP because much of the production within the country accrues to foreigners — the companies we assiduously seek to bring in. Haughton estimates that this foreign element comprises about 12 per cent of the GDP. GDP is probably also overstated in Ireland, since transnational corporations have an interest in making their profits appear to originate in Ireland, because it is a low-tax area for them.

> This can be achieved by underpricing the inputs which Irish subsidiaries buy from affiliates abroad, or by overvaluing the exports which the Irish subsidiaries sell to foreign affiliates (p. 29).

Secondly, foreign transfers such as structural funds to Ireland may have inflated the GDP.

Therefore, for a dispassionate analysis of prosperity, GNP is clearly preferable to GDP. However a further adjustment to the GNP is required to arrive at the GNDI (gross national disposable income). Trade factors or export prices relative to import prices need to be included — Ireland's exports may increase in volume but if these products are worth less because of declining world demand, then the GNP will overstate the purchasing power of Irish incomes. Haughton argued that while real GDP rose by 8.3 per cent annually from 1995–97, this remarkable rate needs to be qualified when thinking about the incomes of Irish people.

> Rising outflows of profits to foreign investors meant that real GNP rose by 7.1 per cent per year; because of falling terms of trade and a slowdown in transfers from the European Union,

> GNDI increased by just 4.6 per cent p.a.; and the immigration
> which was sparked by this recent rise in prosperity ensured
> that the rise in GNDI per capita was just 3.3 per cent per
> year. (p. 30)

From 8.3 per cent to 3.3 per cent, with a few semantic changes? We
still have growth with either figure, but the difference is startling if
one thinks of these figures in relation to, say, a £300 wage per week.
An addition of 3.3 per cent means £9.90 per week while 8.3 per cent
means an additional £24.90.

A different (and Euro-)sceptical analysis is provided in Anthony
Sweeney's colourfully titled book *Irrational Exuberance: The Myth of
the Celtic Tiger* (1999). (Apparently the phrase "Irrational Exuberance" was first used by Alan Greenspan, the director of the US Federal Reserve to decry the overconfidence of people in growing
economies.) Sweeney attacks some prevailing perceptions about
growth in the Irish economy. Approaching the Irish economy from
the position of an orthodox economist, he argues that all the signs of
an up-cycle in business approaching its peak in a classic boom–bust
scenario are plainly visible. While the underlying Irish economy is reasonably strong and has some competitive advantages over its neighbours, many claims about the economy are froth, and often hyped by
those with an interest in maintaining a consumer boom, such as auc-
tioneers and stockbrokers. Serious obstacles to continued controlla-
ble growth have not been confronted. These include loss of control
over the interest rate because of European monetary union (and a
corresponding inappropriately low rate that has fuelled a spending
"bubble"), spectacularly poor infrastructure, the tension for Irish
policy-makers between "pro-business Anglo-Saxon" countries (e.g.
the US and the UK) and pro-social continental countries (such as
Germany and France), the unforeseen consequences of a single currency and the expansion of the European Union. Increasing prosperity itself may paradoxically undermine future prosperity as workers
become less accustomed to making themselves "flexible" and opportunities for easy profits decline. However, while Sweeney sees the
down-cycle as imminent, he does not dispute the growth of the Irish

economy in the last decade and accepts that people's lives did materially and substantially improve in that period, despite the hype.

Kieran Allen's (2000) neo-Marxist critique looks, at least initially, to be a little more serious for an analysis of the relationship between national well-being and prosperity, since it challenges the universality of benefit in the light of the boom. This has clear repercussions for an inquiry that seeks to examine the impact of widespread growth in a society on its members' psyches. If an economy grew by whopping double-figures every year but only, say, 20 per cent of the population enjoyed this growth, then general changes in social values as a consequence might not be anticipated. In other words, if the intention is to examine the general impact of economic change, we must reassure ourselves that the impact of economic change was actually general. Leftists are, of course, notoriously, chronically, pessimistic about economic progress. Although they will accept, under pressure, that the inevitable immiseration of the poor under capitalism is a "vulgarisation" of Marxism, they cannot help talking a fairly similar line — that the working class are the inescapable losers of economic downturns and yet are bypassed in boom times.

Allen's book, *The Celtic Tiger and the Myth of Social Partnership*, attacks the "never had it so good" rhetoric, or argues that it is true but solely for the rich. The Irish economy has grown but has benefited only the employer class. Tax on profits has decreased while the share of the national economy going to profits, interest dividends and rent has increased from 31 per cent in 1987 to 41 per cent in 2000. At the same time, the cut taken by "working people" in terms of wages, pensions and social welfare has declined from 69 per cent to 50 per cent. QED — the rich are getting richer and the poor are getting poorer. Furthermore, the rich have spent their money on an orgy of share speculation while fantastic profits have been repatriated to US multinationals. The Irish government, facilitated by a perfidious trade union leadership, have let the moneyed classes run wild by creating a low-tax, high-profit, relatively deregulated economic island within the EU. Rather than using the profits of the boom to improve conditions for the people by investing in infrastructure, the creaking health system, the ancient rail system, and decent salaries for teachers and nurses, political instincts have been almost viscerally right-wing — reduce the tax burden, forget R&D investment, to hell with health care, f**k the poor, pop open the bubbly, and of course build more and bigger roads (every good Thatcherite loves roads).

It's a strong argument and actually not far off the mark. Certainly, Fianna Fáil's finance maestro, Charlie McCreevy, is ideological about finance and taxation in a way that is not typical of that party's traditions. Irish political rhetoric has sounded increasingly closer, as the current Tánaiste put it, to Boston than to Brussels, presumably meaning that confused sentimentality about the poor should not get in the way of healthy profits (see Chapter 12 for a further discussion of this tension). But Allen's argument understates the degree to which organisations representing the poor were brought on board as social partners. These organisations reported themselves pleased with government policy following the conclusion of Partnership 2000 and PPF. It also fails to acknowledge how much of the demand for tax reduction, the need for reinvestment in the country notwithstanding, came from PAYE workers and that the political instincts of the majority of the Irish people, not just the elite, are rightist.

Most importantly, a leftist critique does not necessarily undermine the argument being pursued in this book. Even if the boom has generated a situation in which the rich have put further "clear blue water" between their position of wealth and that of the average industrial worker and/or the poorest section of society, it is difficult to dispute that the workers have not had material gains in the boom through increased wages. True, there may be a strong case that sections of working people, both in urban and rural areas, have had a *relative* decline of wealth in comparison to the top earners but in *absolute* terms, all have increased, rich and poor alike. In other words, the rich may be taking a larger slice of the pie but that pie itself has grown enormously. (See Chapter 11 for a further discussion of the relative versus absolute debate.) And there are a lot more workers enjoying this enlarged pie. The psychological benefits of increased employment security as well as the reduced threat of forced "welfarisation" or emigration should not be overlooked at the same time.

Overall, this chapter has sought to tease out the actual material improvements people have enjoyed in Ireland as a consequence of the boom. The key point is to beware the hype — we started from a low point as a peripheral European economy; only relatively poor societies grow at the kind of rates claimed for the 1990s in Ireland. The boom has been built on a number of factors, such as an educated workforce, but we're not as well educated as we'd like to think. There are more prosaic reasons for our attractiveness, such as a traditionally flexible and eager workforce and a low corporation tax environment (that does little to enamour us to our fellow EU countries). The degree to which the economy has grown must be carefully assessed, especially to avoid the distortions of the creative accounting practices of multinationals. EU payments and other additions to measurements of economic growth must be weighed up, as must the increasing population sharing the expansion. The scale at which greater money has translated into more comfortable lives has rightly been questioned.

But it must be accepted — regardless of the necessary qualifications to the claim and despite the now obviously transitory nature of the boom — that Irish society and Irish people (to greater and lesser degrees) are a good deal richer and more secure than they were 15 years ago. We may be still grumbling about what we have but protests on a national scale were much less despairing in the 1990s than in, say, the great tax marches of the 1980s or the quiet resignation of emigration throughout the twentieth century. The question to be asked is what has it meant, or done to us as a people and in what ways have we been affected by the new material comfort. In the next chapter, the different places in which we might look for change are outlined through two competing models.

Chapter Four

MODELS OF AFFLUENCE

"In the days when you were
hopelessly poor
I just liked you more"
— The Smiths, "Half a Person"

Wealthy or Rich?

I reviewed the evidence in the last chapter and concluded that, despite the hype, the sceptical leftists, the begrudging rightists and the unbearable smugness, Ireland is a wealthier country than it was 15 or 20 years ago. Even bearing in mind the various caveats — it should have been wealthy anyway, a recession is approaching very quickly, much of the wealth has been mismanaged, and undoubtedly a large chunk of the population has missed out on the benefits — it remains the case, relatively, absolutely and incontrovertibly, that this is a richer country than it was. Or maybe I should stick with "wealthier" — "richer" has many connotations, beyond simply that of being better off financially. The question is what this has done to, and for, us. Are we simply wealthier, purely in financial terms with more goods at our disposal? Or are we a "richer" people — in the sense that, along with more money, we are also richer in wisdom, tolerance, appreciation for democratic institutions, and less philistine, parochial or petty?

And surely that is what's important — the ways in which we've changed and grown with our new wealth. Has it meant nothing more than better bank balances and flasher cars? Or have we used it as the means to greater ends, and developed as a people because of it? This is the acid test of our economic growth — if we have failed to mature, if we're the same people despite it all, then we stand indicted. With some amusement, it was reported in the press some time ago that Irish people were on average a stone heavier than they had been ten years previously. There were ripples of journalistic excitement over the revelation that bra sizes had expanded in line with the economy. But of course, it would be a great shame if an expansion of our bodies and bra sizes rather than our horizons and minds were the only consequence of our productivity, years of work, and patient waiting. That would make us the biggest boobs of all.

Positive and Negative Theories of Change

How does one begin assessing these issues of social-psychological development? Where should one begin to look? A model or theory of change is required to make sense of the many ways in which a national psyche can change during the process of economic growth. The beauty of a theory is that it makes predictions about how and why a transformation might take place and where evidence for that change might be sought. We're in luck, as it happens, since two relevant models are at hand. Better still, they make opposing predictions about the nature of change in times of prosperity. Both are written by North Americans in the second half of the twentieth century — and it's hardly surprising that US[1] thinkers are prone to reflecting on the nature of wealth given their country's economic dominance. In fact, both models emerged in the third quarter of the twentieth century and their concerns reflect (often explicitly and always implicitly) the sensational growth of the US economy following the Second World War and prior to the oil crisis of 1974.

The Positive View 1 — Maslow's Contribution

The first model is based on the writings of Abraham Maslow, a psychologist in the humanist tradition, and his work can be interpreted to suggest that economic prosperity has general and genuine benefits for a society, beyond simply the acquisition of more goods and services. Maslow's best-known book appeared in its first edition in 1954

---

[1] In fact, while J.K. Galbraith has spent virtually all of his adult life in the US, he grew up in a rural part of Canada.

and was entitled *Motivation and Personality*. The argument contained therein is breathtaking in its ambition. By relying on research from a number of different disciplines as well as his own clinical observations, Maslow proposed a general theory of human motivation. In other words, he attempted to formulate a model or hierarchical picture of how we, by which I mean all human beings, are motivated. In the course of this, he outlined the needs that individuals try to satisfy. Of course, we possess, or have the potential to possess, an almost infinite set of needs or desires (e.g. at any given time I may wish for power, fame, a glass of good Bordeaux, a cheeseburger, a better car, hot sex, an interesting picture to look at, a good book, and so on). Maslow's insight was twofold, simple and ingenious — to group all needs into (five) sets and then to rank order these sets.

The Maslowian argument is that people are motivated to act in order to pursue different groups of needs but that they tend to the most urgent needs first — those that are essential for survival. The most important and primary concern that we have is ready access to substances required for basic physiological processes — oxygen, water, protein, sugar and salt to maintain a constant normal blood stream. In other words, without air, water and food, life is unsustainable and, quite sensibly, human beings have evolved to prioritise these essentials before all else. If a person who is missing everything in life must choose which needs or desires to fulfil, then his/her major motivation is to respond to the basic needs rather than any higher-order or more sophisticated ones. As Maslow put it,

> . . . if all the needs are unsatisfied, and the organism is then dominated by the physiological needs, all the other needs may become simply nonexistent . . . the urge to write poetry, the desire to acquire an automobile, the interest in American history, the desire for a new pair of shoes are, in the extreme case, forgotten . . . For the man who is extremely and dangerously hungry, no other interests exist but food. He dreams food, he remembers food, he thinks about food, he emotes only about food, he perceives only food and he wants only food. (Second edition, p. 37)

If people lack the basics, then concern for anything else is a useless luxury, since life cannot go on. To the very hungry, heaven is a place of endlessly abundant food.

Once the core physiological needs have been dealt with though, new and higher desires emerge and possess the organism once more. Maslow suggests that priority is given to safety issues when the basic needs are reasonably well gratified. By safety issues, he was referring to a broad set of concerns about security, stability, protection, order, and freedom from anxiety and chaos. The same characteristics hold true as in the case of the "lowest" needs. The person can be totally dominated by concerns about being secure and safe if she feels none. To a person under constant threat and danger, the requirement of safety dominates and everything else looks less important than safety.

But in an orderly, properly run, modern, stable society, individuals usually feel free from the threat of murder, regular criminal assault, wild animals, chaos, etc. And at this point, the person can become concerned with still higher order needs. "Just as a sated man no longer feels hungry, a safe man no longer feels endangered" (p. 41). The next priority, Maslow proposed, was the need for belonging and love. People who experience no threat to life either by shortage of resources or lack of security will begin to pine for friends, family, loved ones. Primo Levi (1988), a survivor of Nazi concentration camps, wrote about his feelings in the few times when his very existence was not under immediate threat. A terrible loneliness swept over him as he remembered all those friends and family now lost. Similarly, Maslow writes that when a man

> . . . was hungry, he sneered at love as unreal or unnecessary . . .
> now [if the basic and safety needs have been resolved] he will
> feel sharply the pangs of loneliness, of ostracism, of rejection.
> (p. 43)

The cycle then operates once more — if these are resolved, the esteem needs become the driving force of the organism. Esteem needs involve both self-respect as well as the respect of others. For self-respect, we need self-confidence, a feeling that we have mastered certain tasks, a sense of adequacy in our actions. For the latter, the respect of others, we look to achieve a certain status within the community that is important to us, perhaps even fame and glory, or at least appreciation and recognition among our peers and friends.

Maslow's final step on the ladder, the highest motivation and one which only comes into play when we feel we have resolved all other threats — i.e., the basic physiological needs, the requirement for security, the desire to feel loved by at least some people, and respected by others — is that which he labels self-actualisation. This is a little vague but is meant to convey the notion of complete fulfilment, of being everything that we can be, of realising our potential. It can vary from person to person — for some, it may be to invent something, for others to be creative artists, for others to be an ideal worker or partner. This hazy notion of self-completion lies at the summit of the motivational forces we will experience but climbing this summit can only be attempted when we have crossed all the lower obstacles.

The Positive View 2 — Inglehart's Social Analogy

Maslow's typology is an account of the basic and higher motivational forces that drive the typical human being. It has a dynamic nature — people are never left permanently contented by the resolution of an important or long-standing need or ambition — rather, the resolution of a lower need reorients them to a new set of challenges or demands. This model obviously refers to the dynamics of a single person or individual. In what way might it be made relevant to interpreting broader change or the transformation of a whole society, such as the consequences of rapid economic transformation in Ireland? It was another thinker, Ronald Inglehart, who sought to apply Maslow's insight to widespread social change and values. (We could call the combined theory the Maslow-Inglehart model, but in the interests of simplicity, let's simply refer to it as the Positive View.) The Positive View conceives of societies changing in the same manner as Maslow proposed individuals did. In other words, Inglehart's original contribution is to hypothesise about the consequences for a society if the basic needs of most of its members are met.

The experience of wealth is very brief for most nations. In the span of human history, apart from a minuscule elite, only a few generations of Europeans and North Americans have not had to concern themselves, as a whole, with worries about food and shelter. Inglehart has argued that the experience of security must be profoundly consequential. Drawing on Maslow's model, he has suggested that just as an individual can concern herself with higher concerns such as the need for love, belonging, self-esteem and self-actualisation only when food and shelter are first provided, so a society will only prioritise democracy, debate, equality, fairness, aesthetic and environmental concerns when employment, law and order, basic housing and income guarantees are first dealt with, at least for the vast majority. In his book *The Silent Revolution*, Inglehart analogised the basic (physiological) and higher (psychological) needs of Maslow's individual with what he calls the basic (materialist) and higher (post-materialist) priorities of a society (see Figure 4.1 below). And he has suggested that in the post-Second World War era, the majority of citizens of Western industrialised countries were presented for the first time with the luxury of preoccupation with post-materialist concerns — no longer worrying about jobs, the threat of war, or the roof over their heads, but of the kind of environments they lived in, of the rights of expression, of the importance of abstract issues like equality, justice and minority rights. For Inglehart, the mass student demonstrations of the 1970s, the demand for gay and ethnic minority rights as well as the rise of Green parties were symptoms of the success of conventional politics in dealing with hunger, unemployment, the threat of homelessness, the fear of chaos and so on. When, for most people, these issues are no longer pressing concerns, because they are experiencing financial security in relatively stable societies, their priorities turn elsewhere — towards freedom, expression, beauty.

Figure 4.1: The Maslow-Inglehart Hierarchy of Needs for Individuals and Societies (from Inglehart, 1977: 42)

	Aesthetic:	• Beautiful cities/nature
Social and self-actualisation needs (Post-materialist)	Intellectual:	• Ideas count • Free speech
	Belonging and esteem:	• Less impersonal society • More say on job, community • More say in government
	Safety needs:	• Strong defence forces • Fight crime • Maintain order
Physiological needs (Materialist)	Sustenance needs:	• Stable economy • Economic growth • Fight rising prices

Inglehart's views have been critiqued and he has modified his position somewhat in *Culture Shift* (1990) and *Modernization and Post-Modernization* (1997). However, he has remained faithful to the basic premise of the Positive View — that higher priorities replace lower ones when those lower ones are resolved and that the modern phenomenon of widespread material comfort in Western societies means that most citizens are focused on post-material concerns relating to "self-expression and quality of life" (1997: 4).

> The term "*Post*-materialist" denotes a set of goals that are emphasized *after* people have attained material security, and *because* they have attained material security. (Inglehart, 1997: 35) [Emphasis in original]

Inglehart summarised his position quite neatly when he argued that we have witnessed a move from "survival" values to "well-being values". When the majority live in poverty, then immediate survival is the foremost priority. The main social-psychological characteristic of survival-oriented societies is that of insecurity. On the other hand, when economic and physical security are no longer to the forefront, as in wealthier societies, well-being and self-expression issues are prioritised (having previously been regarded as luxuries) now that people feel secure. Thus Inglehart presents us with a dichotomy: poor, materialist, insecure societies, where survival is prioritised, versus wealthier, post-materialist, secure societies, where well-being and quality of life are stressed. Insecure and secure societies differ from one another, it is proposed, in certain predictable ways. People try to resolve the sensation of physical insecurity in poorer societies by finding security elsewhere — thus, their politics reflect the need for strong leaders, for order and unquestionable authority. An intolerance of change and difference is reflected in hostility towards immigrants and ethnic minorities (see Chapter 7). Under conditions of insecurity, people are more willing to subordinate their own goals to the existing social order and idiosyncrasy and self-expression are not valued. In the face of economic uncertainty, existential certainty is prized and absolute and unbending religious rules and fundamentalist dogma are the norm. Economically, growth is prioritised above all else; unshackled, unqualified and unquestioning material expansion becomes the order of the day. Because the nuclear heterosexual family is usually the key economic unit of the poorer society, then any threat to it and its optimal reproductive power from such diverse phenomena as the availability of divorce, abortion and contraception and the adoption of homosexual and alternative lifestyles, are at best frowned upon and often criminalised.

On the other hand, in secure societies, post-materialist values are emergent. There is a shift away from authority in general, in either its religious or political expressions and absolutism is not only de-emphasised but challenged. There is no longer the need for strict unbending rules and post-materialists, "raised under conditions of relative security, can tolerate more ambiguity" (1997: 40). Post-materialists, their physical security assured, are better able to look critically at the values and norms they live by. Rules are no longer black and white; people understand the existence of grey areas and can apply moral codes selectively and flexibly. Respect for authority declines and erodes; there is a greater demand for widespread participation in the making of decisions. Loyalties to political parties and established religions decline. Xenophobia is less widespread in more secure societies and the exotic and different are more highly valued. In work, people are no longer satisfied with simply earning enough to keep themselves and family in food and a house — they want to have more meaningful and intellectually demanding jobs while the challenge to hierarchy means they also want a say in how the workplace is managed and organised. The economic functionality of the older rigid family structure is weakened and there is a greater tolerance of gays and lesbians as well as single-parent families. The decline of religion is matched ironically by a *growth* in spirituality as people spend more time thinking about the meaning and purpose of their existence outside rigid religious structures.

Problems with the Positive View

That is the Positive View in a nutshell — the theory that material growth enhances societies well beyond simply providing more jobs, cars and chickens in every pot. The wealthy society in the Maslow-Inglehart model, if not The Good Society, is certainly evolving in the right direction at the very least. There is a nice intuitive feel and logic to the argument. But does it stand up to scrutiny? Inglehart has used survey data to examine the plausibility of his claims and in later chapters here, the same will be done in an Irish context. But aside from survey data, what about the general claim — that societies are better places when they are wealthier? The world is certainly richer and more secure for a larger number of people than ever before but are we richer, as people, for it? Historically, the case looks shaky. The civil progress of early capitalism gave way to the horror in the last century of fascism and concentration camps, but standards of living had surely improved. As an example of declining standards, the revolutionary, Friedrich Engels, was sympathetic to the political aspirations of the Fenians in the nineteenth century but was shocked by their "terrorist" tactics in Britain and the threat to civilian life. (What would Engels have made of the spectacular atrocities in the US on 11 September 2001?) Are there any countries now in the advanced West where terrorists have not bombed at will, indifferent to, or at least accepting of civilian losses? Greater inhumanity, not humanity, has been on show, it can easily be argued, in the twentieth century.

Eric Hobsbawm (1994) proposed that increased wealth and barbarism in fact blossomed together in the twentieth century — from the aerial bombing of civilians by the nationalists in the Spanish Civil War, the French use of electric shock torture in the Algerian War, to US-backed genocide in Latin America under Reagan in the 1980s. And while there was terrible suffering in older, poorer times,[2] simultaneous food overproduction *and* indifference to hunger elsewhere is a decidedly modern phenomenon in developed countries.

The Positive View suggests that we can turn to self-expression and self-actualisation when other goals have been answered, but does any cultural historian seriously believe that the artists, writers or dramatists in Western countries in the second half of the twentieth century (the wealthier half, when the Golden Age of Capitalism occurred) were superior to those of the first half of the century (the poorer, unstable half) — think Eliot, Joyce and Picasso versus Hughes, Flann O'Brien and Warhol? Or that the twentieth century, the high point of economic productivity, was also the high point of creative expression? Middle America certainly does not lack material comfort, but the degree to which its main goal is self-expression is questionable (unless we're counting the "my mom seduced my gay cat" style of self-expression on daytime TV). And aren't great artists meant to be poor and live in garrets anyway? Are political revolution and unrest not usually accompanied by revolutionary forms of art and thinking?

---

[2] And terrible mundane cruelties — Norbert Elias (1978) described how all sections of society, including children, were encouraged to enjoy the rituals of public cat-burning in sixteenth-century Paris.

The Negative View — Galbraith

Caution must thus be exercised before celebrating the new human being. The Positive View may still be correct, but it is by no means an open-and-shut case. One of the sharpest exponents of what I will call the Negative View is John Kenneth Galbraith. Galbraith is an original thinker and populariser of economic ideas, a towering intellect and above all a writer of great vision, intelligence and humour. He has been a long-time advocate of the important role of the state in directing modern economies and, for his opponents, a formidable critic of free market dogmas. One of his best-known works was entitled *The Affluent Society*, the first edition of which appeared in 1958. In this book, he analysed the nature of the then-buoyant US economy. The publication date is important, since this was a high-point of the Golden Age of Capitalism and many of the anxieties of the time related to problems of success — just as many do in Ireland today.

Galbraith's position is not anti-growth; what he does question are the ends to which the productive capacities of affluent societies are directed. He agrees with one part of the Positive View — that people who are engaged in a daily struggle for sheer survival tend not to be overly concerned with more subtle goals. In the past, food, clothes and shelter were in scarce supply and were at the centre of people's thoughts. Where Galbraith breaks from the Positive View is in his belief that when goods become abundant, we do not necessarily change our priorities to other higher goals such as love and self-actualisation. In fact, we often try to express these higher psychological needs *through* our patterns of consumption. More specifically, Galbraith was interested in social life in the US of the post-war era when, for most people, goods were abundant.

> Although there is malnutrition, more die in the United States of too much food than of too little. Where the population was once thought to press on the food supply, now . . . the food supply presses on the population. (1969, 2nd edition, p. 118)

But Galbraith argued that people remained preoccupied with the production of goods even when the steel needed for cars was purely decorative or when the production of clothes no longer had any simple functionality such as for protection but was almost exclusively for fashionable, expressive or erotic purposes. This widespread and continuing obsession with production in already over-productive societies is neither healthy nor "natural" or innate. Rather, Galbraith saw it as a deliberate policy of producers to promote a certain materialist or consumerist ideology:

> . . . so all embracing is our sense of the importance of production as a goal that the first reaction to any questioning of this attitude will be "What else is there?" So large does production bulk in our thoughts that we can only suppose that a vacuum must remain if it should be relegated to a smaller role. (p. 119)

For Galbraith, the troubling characteristic of the affluent society is that, by its very nature, production cannot lead to a reduction in people's wants. The reason is that one of the main goals is to keep at least abreast but preferably ahead of one's neighbour. So, having goods alone can never quench people's desires — what they want is relative success in comparison to others and this success is measured by the goods they have. The vicious circle inherent in this model is clear:

> The notion of independently established need now sinks into the background. . . . Because the society sets great store by ability to produce a high living standard, it evaluates people by the products they possess. The more that is produced, the more that must be owned. (pp. 148–149)

Modern advertising, it is suggested, is the mechanism by which consumer knowledge is not merely enhanced but rather the way in which consumer desire is created. Incidentally, this substantially pre-dates Naomi Klein's (2000) claim that producers sell autonomous brand identities instead of goods. As Galbraith noted four decades earlier, the consumer is

> . . . subject to the forces of advertising and emulation by which production creates its own demand. Advertising operates exclusively, and emulation mainly, on behalf of privately produced goods and services. (p. 230)

Rather than leading to the development of a healthier community, the artificial promotion of personal consumption and privileged ownership leads to massive distortions in the affluent society. The startling stress on the importance of privately produced goods creates an imbalance and publicly rendered services are completely overlooked and left to wither. Reflect on Galbraith's description of life in the affluent society: on the one hand,

> the schools were old and overcrowded . . . the parks and playgrounds were insufficient. . . . Access to the city by those who work there was uncertain and painful and becoming more so. Internal transportation was overcrowded, un-healthful and dirty. So was the air . . . deficiencies were not in new and novel services but in old and established ones . . . this public poverty competed with the stories of ever-increasing opulence in privately produced goods. The Gross National Product was rising. So were retail sales. So was personal in-come. . . . The automobiles that could not be parked were being produced at an expanded rate. . . . The children, dis-posed to increasingly imaginative forms of delinquency, were admirably equipped with television sets. (p. 222)

The description is of 1950s New York but is strongly reminiscent of more recent attempts by Frank McDonald or Ann Marie Hourihane to capture the phenomenon of the Celtic Tiger at the end of the last decade.

Galbraith offers the following sketch to push the point home:

> The family which takes its mauve and cerise, air-conditioned, power-steered and power-braked automobile out for a tour passes through cities that are badly paved, made hideous by litter, blighted buildings, billboards and posts for wires that should long since have been put underground. . . . They picnic on exquisitely packaged food from a portable icebox by a polluted stream and go on to spend the night at a park which is a menace to public health and morals. Just before dozing off, amid the stench of decaying refuse, they reflect vaguely on the curious unevenness of their blessings. (p. 223)

In Galbraith's view, increased production does not necessarily liber-ate people from material concerns. On the contrary, its damning characteristic is a value system that promotes the desire to own more and better objects than anyone else. The advertising system works in tandem to ensure that satisfaction of certain material needs, rather than diverting people away from material concerns, leads to a demand for more. Thus materialism begets more materialism, not post-materialism. Again, the originality of Galbraith's work is such that his ideas are still being "rediscovered" in consumer psychology — the psychologist Robert E. Lane (2000) has written of the "hedonistic treadmill" — the more you have, the more you want. With an initial increase of wealth, the formerly poor feel a real benefit. However, further rises in goods and pay fail to bring the same pleasure and people want more. Thus materialism grows and crowds out other values.

The Ambiguous Quality of Progress

> Constant revolutionising of production, uninterrupted disturbance of all social conditions, everlasting uncertainty and agitation distinguish the bourgeois epoch from all earlier ones. . . . All that Is solid melts into air, all that is holy is profaned, and man is at last compelled to face, with sober senses, his real conditions of life, and his relations with his kind. (Marx and Engels, *Manifesto of the Communist Party*)

It is always surprising to recall the degree to which Marx despised capitalism while also recognising its great revolutionary force, as it split apart the old order in Europe. In a more geographically limited context (Ireland) and temporally circumscribed manner (the late 1980s to the beginning of the twenty-first century), the purpose of the remaining chapters is to seek to investigate the complex set of impacts of radical economic change on society and its institutions. The Positive View and the Negative View have been outlined and provide competing hypotheses about change and direct us to areas where we might look for that change. According to the Positive View, sustained economic growth and the security thus provided enable a society to go beyond their material concerns and dogmatic beliefs and advance towards better self-expression, sophisticated and abstract concerns about democracy and equality, spirituality and freedom, quality of life issues such as the nature of our cities and environment as well as a rejection of close-minded absolutist thinking. In the Negative View, materialism generates a further cycle of crass materialism, a selfish obsession with owning more and bigger products and a craving for personal largesse at the expense of the wider public good.

Marx also suggested that history repeats itself (first as a tragedy, then as a farce). Are we reliving the 1980s Thatcherite boom in Ireland now or are we maturing into a society where freedom and wisdom rule? To return to the question posed in the opening of this chapter, are we richer or just wealthier? The analysis is directed towards answering this question by reviewing the available evidence in Ireland in various domains (sexuality, politics, consumption, art and leisure, as well as the fates of different sections of the population).

Modernisation

One other complication raises its head. Ireland has changed because of economic development, no doubt, and the goal is to try to evaluate the nature of that change. But of course, time has also moved on, and it exerts its own pressure. No one can doubt that, regardless of fiscal trends, Ireland could not have been the same country now, say, as in 1985. There are longer-term trends at play and one must be careful not to wrongly attribute these trends to economic causes, rather than to broader historical forces. Sociologists like Weber noted that modernisation led to increased "individualisation", whereby values are no longer dominated by certain institutions, especially religious, and are now increasingly based on personal choice. Thus, modernisation brings with it a move away from traditional value systems and toward secularisation, increased pluralism in ideas, greater levels of emancipation, bureaucratisation (or rational planning) and demystification (the decline of superstition and growing emphasis on practical rationality and predictability). These sociological processes were already occurring in the 1980s, although in a comparatively sluggish way. Church authority was being weakened before the period of rapid economic growth and the strong secularising influence of Britain was never absent from our culture or thinking. The importance of values promoting "me and mine" as opposed to "us and ours" is not unique to the present. It will be essential to tease apart the direct consequences of new money as well as the playing out of forces already in motion. Putting it crudely, Ireland has got bigger and older at the same time and it is hoped that we can assess its level of maturity and in that context evaluate its behaviour.

Chapter 5

CONFESSIONS OF A LAPSED CATHOLIC NATION

Roma locuta est; causa finita[1]

In Chapter 2, evidence was presented demonstrating the salience of religious belief in traditional Irish society — or the salience of religious ritual and institutions at any rate. In sociological terms, Ireland's love affair with Catholic institutions has been, frankly, totally OTT. Public displays of affection between people and church were constant and blatant, regardless of the presence of outsiders. They were never out of each other's company. It was a case of complete mutual obsession. (Even the Italians were beginning to gossip.) In the neutral language of social science, Ireland was a statistical outlier in comparison to other developed countries. As sociologist Tony Fahey (1992) put it, "Irish commitment to institutional catholicism remains quite exceptional by western standards" (p. 303), which incidentally, is a polite way of saying weird. Of course, there's nothing more relative than weirdness . . .

Nic Ghiolla Phádraig (1986) reminds us of the tangible forms of the weirdness, some still around, some disappearing:

> . . . the Angelus on TV, the sober-clad clergy and religious symbols everywhere — in jewellery, in propaganda on justice and morality, in religious imagery (both devout and blasphemous) and in speech. (p. 139)

---

[1] Rome has spoken, the case is closed.

In a later article (1995), she noted:

> Ireland's religious profile is unusual in a number of respects. It
> is the only country in the English-speaking world which has a
> Catholic majority. It is unique among western countries in not
> permitting divorce and abortion. Ireland is also unusual . . . in
> that the main proportion of the population regularly practise
> religion. (p. 593)

A frequently used piece of archive material is recordings of the Eucharistic Congress in 1932 in Ireland. John McCormack, papal count of the Holy Roman Empire, sang and the masses prostrated themselves, quite literally. A year earlier in Spain, revolutionary workers had burned churches and convents to the ground (in refusing to call out the civil guard, the leftist Minister of War declared that "all the convents in Madrid are not worth the life of one Republican"). Little of the anti-clerical fervour so common in other developed countries with a dominant Catholic church ever occurred in Ireland. We remained the saints, if not the scholars, of Europe.

The theme of this book is recent change in Ireland. The specific question posed in this chapter is the impact of the recent past, particularly of rapidly changing economic and social circumstances, on religious belief and observation. Nic Ghiolla Phadraig cites the phenomenon of weekly religious attendance as a reasonable measure by which to assess change. The Eurobarometer and ISSP data sets are heavily relied on here to assess religious conviction and behaviour — see descriptive note at the end of Chapter 1.

Holier than Thou (or Them)

One regular question posed in the Eurobarometer survey is frequency of church attendance. A brief review of the figures reveals that in Ireland, the opium of the masses was, fittingly, mass. In 1975, a representative and large sample of individuals from all (then nine) EEC member states were asked about their frequency of church attendance. The very devout group, who selected "several times" per week, was largest in Ireland at 18.0 per cent, nearly one in five. The nearest to this (apart from Northern Ireland with 14.5 per cent) were the respondents from Luxembourg — less than one in ten.

However, it is only by adding those attending "several times a week" with those going "weekly" that Ireland's unusual religiosity becomes really apparent. The figure for Ireland — attending a church service at least once a week — was 89.1 per cent, while the equivalent for Denmark (at the other extreme) is 4.8 per cent. Between those poles are Great Britain at 14.9 per cent, France with 17.3 per cent, West Germany at 22.3 per cent and Italy at 35.4 per cent. The contrast could hardly be greater — behaviour that was absolutely normal and standard in Ireland was that of a (sometimes very small) minority in other societies. In Figure 5.1 below, the figures of church attendance for the then EEC average (excluding Ireland) and Ireland are displayed.

Figure 5.1: Religious Attendance — Ireland and the EEC (1975)

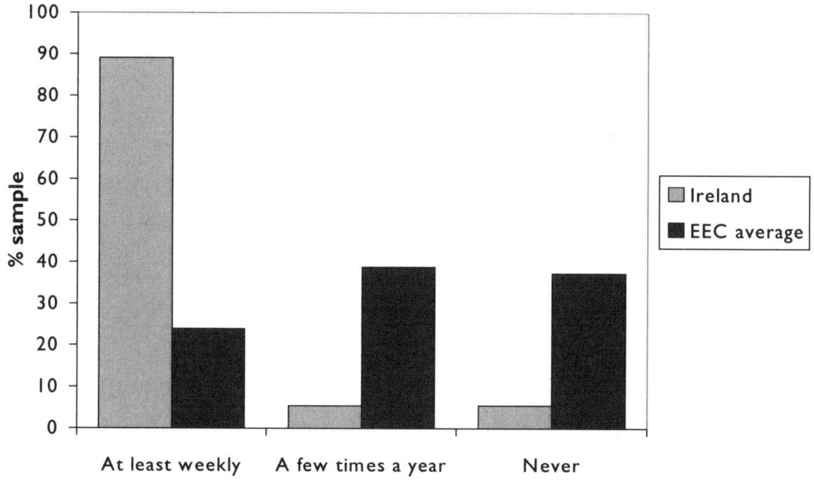

Source: Eurobarometer

The standard pattern elsewhere was a rough three-way split between the very or fairly devout, the occasional attenders (best typified in the tradition of French Catholicism, with more than 40 per cent of that country's sample going "a few times a year") and the non- or anti-religious. In Ireland, that pattern completely broke down and, instead, all bar a tiny minority were to be found at the Sabbath service. Of course, attendance isn't everything. The Pharisees, it will be remembered, were sticklers for orthodox behaviour while lacking genuine integrity. It is possible that one might attend a service in a casual way (or even treat it as a social event) while remaining fairly indifferent to its religious message. But the Eurobarometer surveys also provide information about people's assessment of the importance of religiosity in their lives. Figure 5.2 below contrasts the percentages for Ireland with the EEC mean in 1975.

Figure 5.2: Importance of Religion to Respondent — Ireland and the EEC (1975)

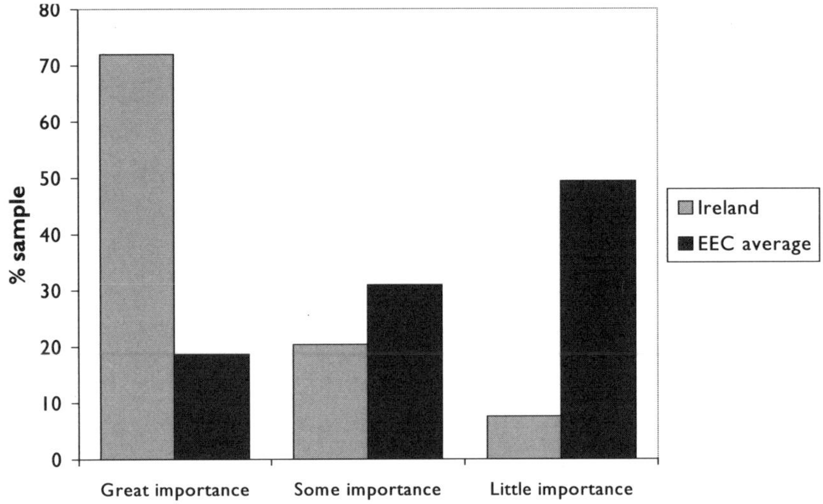

Source: Eurobarometer

Again, the pattern typical elsewhere is reversed with almost chemical precision in Ireland. Nearly everyone attended a religious service (and almost all of these are Catholic services) and religion was perceived to be of great importance in people's lives. No doubt it was. We were the Holy Joes of the EEC. How can this ultra-religiosity be explained without recourse to circular arguments (e.g. the Irish are naturally religious)?

Fahey (1992) has suggested that nationalism and Catholicism became bound up together in the late nineteenth century to produce a "national Catholicism".

> In spite of the contribution of Irish protestant tradition to nationalist politics, national identity was tied up with rejection of the protestantism of the British state and increasingly came to

> be expressed in an effusive identification with catholicism and
> the Catholic Church. (p. 305)

The high number of priests proportional to the population at the
end of the nineteenth century — a situation caused partly for ideological reasons and partly for economic ones, e.g. the families of large
farmers wanted to have at least one son in the priesthood — meant
that the need for lay participation in the administration and organisation of the church was low, relative to other Catholic European
countries. The energies of abundantly available religious females
were directed into the social service work of education, health and
orphanages. Fahey also suggests that the strongly "devotional" nature of Irish Catholicism — expressed in mass attending — was a
consequence of the "unique degree" of control over the educational
system, in comparison to other countries. This system was

> . . . the church's principal instrument for catechetical instruc-
> tion and . . . undoubtedly an important vehicle for the doc-
> trinal revolution. (p. 307)

The sectioning off of the Protestant tradition into the six counties
and successive governments of a conservative nationalist bent in the
Free State consolidated the power of an increasingly unchallenged,
and unchallengeable, Catholic church. Fahey argues that the rise of
liberalism in the 1960s along with modernisation following the Second Vatican Council modified the pre-eminence of Catholicism,
without really undermining it. Thus, even in 1975, nine in ten people
in Ireland, overwhelmingly Catholic, attended at least one weekly
religious service.

A Drifting Flock

What has happened since 1975? Most observers have noted that,
despite increased urbanisation in Ireland, the process of secularisation was occurring very slowly and the Catholic church kept most of
its flock intact. However, more recent figures reveal that things are
changing rapidly. Using Eurobarometer data at three later points —
1985, 1991 and 1999, the drift from the highpoint of 1975 becomes
clear (see Figure 5.3).

Figure 5.3: Declining Percentage Attending Weekly Religious Service in Ireland

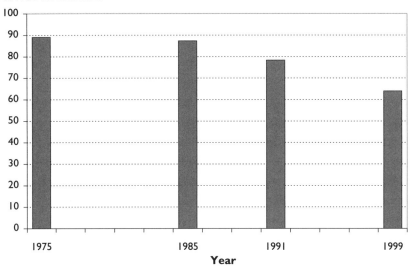

Source: Eurobarometer

The percentages in Figure 5.3 are quite instructive. They reveal that the decline of regular church attenders was barely discernible as late as 1985, where the reduction might even be due to sampling error. However, the 14 years between 1985 and 1999 witnessed a decline of 23.4 per cent in absolute terms. This meant that every year, there were almost two per cent fewer attending than in the previous year and the rate appears to be accelerating. Two per cent a year may not sound like very much but even if that rate of decline stayed constant and if the figure of around 64 per cent were accurate for 1999, then by 2007, weekly mass-goers would be an absolute minority of the Irish population for the first time since the famine.

An interesting comparison might be made with British politics. The historian Dangerfield proposed that liberalism was in mortal danger in England paradoxically when it looked most strong — after the overwhelming triumph of the Liberals in the 1906 election, a victory "from which they never recovered" (1935: 21). In the same way, the political power of the Catholic Church in Ireland looked complete after the defeat of the divorce referendum in 1986. And yet it is now clear that that victory was its last great show of strength, its last hurrah.

Why the rapid decline in both mass attendance and mass support? Sociological models predict a general decline of religious belief as societies modernise quite simply through secularisation — "the process whereby religious thinking, practice and institution lose social significance" (Wilson, 1966: xiv). Wallis and Bruce argue that religion declines during the process of modernisation unless it "finds or retains work to do other than relating individuals to the supernatural" (1992: 17). General modernisation and secularisation are almost certainly relevant for the very long-term view of Irish society, but they do not provide an elegant explanation of the sharp change from the late 1980s to the present.

Are there models that fit the trends more neatly? In answering, it is important to distinguish between events and processes. Events are those occurrences that make the news. Processes, on the other hand, occur over the medium to long term, across years and decades. Two explanations have been offered for the decline of religiosity among the Irish public — one event-based and the other process-based. The event-based explanation proposes that high-profile scandals involving individual members of the church ranging from the horrific (the protection offered by the church to sexual abusers such as Brendan Smyth and Sean Fortune) to the merely hypocritical (the conservative moralising of Eamonn Casey and Michael Cleary in contrast to their lifestyles) fatally undermined the trust of the Irish people in the Catholic church. An alternative version of this, where the liberal media is said to have sensationalised the actions of a few bad apples, is occasionally bandied about by the more brazen members of the clergy. However, the event-based explanation is unattractive in several ways. Experimental psychologists have shown that people have ways of bracketing off exceptions to the rule, when they want to, and thus should surely be able to distinguish between the corrupt behaviour of some individuals and the root-and-branch corruption of an entire organisation. Nor do the data fit a "sudden loss of belief" model in the institution of the Catholic church. Another survey series, the ISSP, has asked people about their religious beliefs in greater

detail. This was done in 1991 and 1998 in Ireland. The contrast between the two dates is instructive. The decline of attendance rates
at church service is again visible. However, people were also asked
to describe the way, if at all, they believed in God. In Figure 5.4, the
three main groupings of belief are shown for data gathered in 1991
and 1998. The "negative" group were those who said they did not
believe in God, or thought that God's existence was unknowable or
that there was some sort of "Higher Power" but not an individual
God. The "intermediate" group believed sometimes but were racked
by serious doubts. The "positive" group believed in God and never
entertained doubts about it.

Figure 5.4: Beliefs in Ireland about the Existence of God, 1991–98

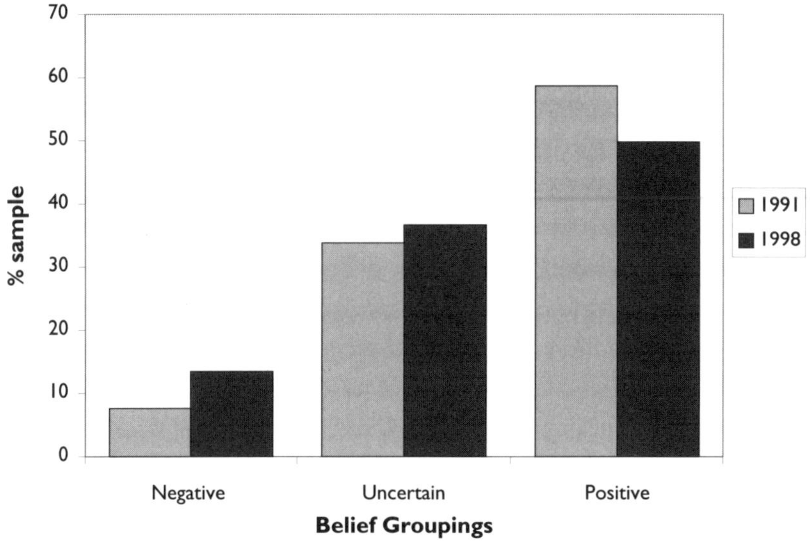

Source: ISSP

As can be seen, the biggest decline is in the positive group while the
non-believers and the intermediate "doubters" were growing. A
theory for declining mass-going which relied on church scandals
might be a logical possibility — disenchantment with the institution
— but does not explain why many people's philosophical or existential beliefs altered as they clearly have over the short period of seven
years. Almost 10 per cent less of the population are now positive
about the existence of God than previously.

A more plausible medium-term process-based explanation is available. The recovery from the economic lowpoint of the 1980s towards the boom of the late 1990s altered the needs of Irish society. Inglehart's model was described in a previous chapter and it provides a social-psychological link between rapid economic growth and social values. Scarcity and insecurity, Inglehart argues, lead people to seek out abundance and certainty. This occurs both at the material level but also at the ideological level whereby the existential security of religious absolutism, even fundamentalism, is reassuring to a population enduring doubts and fears about their political and economic viability. However, substantial material growth assuages the concerns of many and they are less attracted to, and less in need of, the inflexibility and dogmatism (but certainty) of religious belief. This is a more elegant explanation of the decline both in belief and behaviour and also why this occurs so steeply during the time of greatest economic certainty. It will be interesting to examine whether the coming economic recession will reverse the decline in strong religious beliefs

Men and Women, Rich and Poor, Old and Young

The Irish population and their religiosity have been treated as a uniform whole so far in this discussion. But of course, differences within a society are also interesting to explore in their own right. These differences — for example between men and women or young and old — and differential levels of religious commitment may also have theoretical relevance in choosing the best explanation for longer-term religious decline.

Sex and religious commitment is an interesting topic. It is sometimes argued, for example, that women's religious commitment "saved" Italy from communism in the post-war era. In 1948, the popular Italian Communist party looked like making an electoral breakthrough and taking power in that country by constitutional means. Close to election day, the priests launched a powerful campaign from the pulpits to command women, it is argued, to persuade their more anti-clerical menfolk from going down the Bolshevist road (see Ginsborg, 1990: Chapter 3). Whatever the importance of these interventions, the perception that women are generally more pious than men, especially in Catholic countries, is widely held.

What about in Ireland? The Eurobarometer surveys again provide information at a number of points in the last three decades. Figure 5.5 presents the rate of church attendance among representative samples of the Irish population.

Figure 5.5: Percentage of Irish Males and Females Attending Weekly Religious Service since 1975

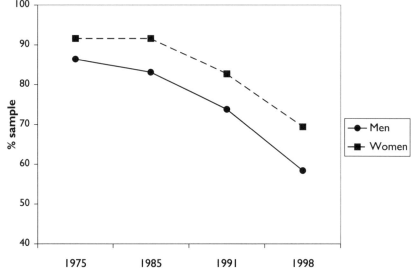

Source: Eurobarometer

As Figure 5.5 indicates, there is some evidence for a small but consistent difference between the sexes in terms of religiosity (at least using weekly church attendance as the critical measure). However, the steady decline among males and females in the percentages attending between 1975 and 1998 are more or less parallel — there is no evidence that men, for example, have given up on God *en masse* while women stay loyal.

Income is another possible factor. It was suggested by some that the victory of the pro-divorce side in the 1995 referendum was due to the Church "losing" its working class constituency. The Eurobarometer surveys provide information on individuals falling into higher and lower income groups. Figure 5.6 contrasts the proportions of both sub-samples attending a weekly church service in 1975 and 1998.

Figure 5.6: Percentage Higher and Lower Income Groups Attending Weekly Church, 1975 and 1998

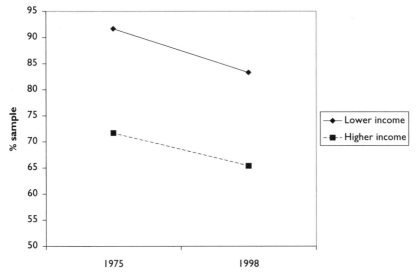

Source: Eurobarometer

Once again, there is evidence for a modest but consistent difference between the income groups and, supportive of Inglehart's line of reasoning, the better-off are less likely to make use of the church on a weekly basis. However, there is no clear evidence that the Church has especially lost its lower income adherents — rather, both income groups continue to drift away at a relatively similar pace.

Finally in this section, we must consider the relationship between age and religiosity. Inglehart has argued that the economic conditions prevailing when one is young may be crucial in shaping later beliefs. (Ageing itself also increases awareness of mortality, of course.) Those whose main experience and memories are of economic failure and political instability are more likely to seek out security in firm religious dogma while those whose environment is one of plenty and prosperity have less need of it. Figure 5.7 presents the rate of church attendance for four age groups at different times.

Figure 5.7: Percentage of Different Age Groups Attending Weekly Church, 1975, 1991, 1998

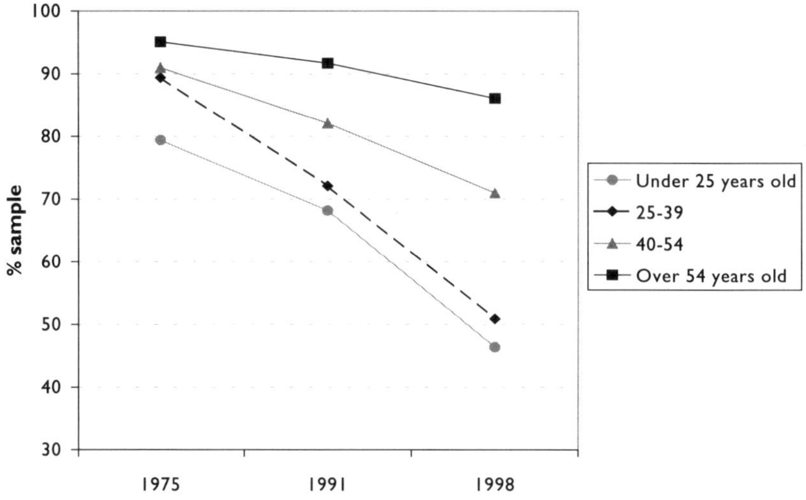

Source: Eurobarometer

A novel and important pattern emerges. There were minor age differences in 1975 but by 1998, they have sharpened considerably. While the passage of 23 years has seen a decline in weekly attendance of about 9 per cent in absolute terms of the oldest group, this is in the order of 33 per cent for the youngest group. Indeed, Irish weekly church-attending under-25 year olds are now a minority of their age group. It is the loss of the younger, supposedly more dynamic, members of society that must be one of the greatest concerns to priests and bishops as they observe their grey-haired faithful on Sunday mornings. The pattern is consistent with Inglehart's prediction — those who either grew up with or spent a greater proportion of their years enjoying the good times are less likely to remain committed to an absolutist rule-based religion. The sharpest drop in attendance has been in the 25–39 age group, probably the main benefactors of economic boom. On the other hand, those whose dominant memories and life experiences were shaped by poverty, uncertainty and the threat of turbulence are more attracted to the demands but also assurances of a belief system like Catholicism.

Believe it or not . . .

It has been argued, in contrast to the analysis presented here, that Ireland has changed little with regard to widespread religious beliefs. For example, the Chicagoan sociologist Fr Andrew Greeley (along with professor Fr Conor Ward) reviewed the findings of the ISSP data for 1998 and

> . . . expressed himself astonished that the young Irish were so profoundly Catholic — "My personal impression from the survey is that the Irish are incorrigibly and irredeemably Catholic," said Greeley. (Quoted in *The Irish Times* on 28 November 2000, based on an article in *Doctrine and Life* (2000))

I think this is an odd interpretation — perhaps there is a clash between what the professors would like to be the case and what a disinterested reader of the data would say. For example, is there anything more incorrigibly Catholic than the practice of prayer (as opposed, for example, to the Calvinist tradition of revealing your piety through actions not words)? In the ISSP survey 1991, 68.2 per cent of respondents claimed to pray at least several times a week (compared to a European average of 30.3 per cent). A mere seven years later, when the 1998 ISSP survey posed the same question, it was found that only 45.2 per cent of individuals now claimed to pray that often.

The professors (Greeley and Ward) do acknowledge that on attitudes to sexual relationships as well as Church authority, there has been a marked decline. However, they argue that the core teachings of the Church are still firmly held by almost as many Irish people as ever. Leaving aside the thorny question of whether people are actually aware of what the core teachings of the Church are, there are a number of problems with this claim. The first is that, as we have seen, the more convincing explanation of the trend is a move away from absolutist or dogmatic belief systems, especially among those who have known a materially better life. For some people, this means an explicit departure from the Catholic church. For many more, the result is the development of a sort of "grey" rather than "black and white" set of beliefs. Thus, we see a development of the kind of "suit yourself" religiosity for which the Church of England is often satirised. This is the sort of *à la carte* Catholicism, as one senior churchman neatly described it, which retains the touchy-feely harmless bits of a belief but omits the rules that might actually impinge on one's life, such as those relating to sexual continence outside marriage for example.

The only survey items which *do* maintain consistency over the two ISSP periods (1991–1998) are quite surprising ones at first glance. Belief in the existence of heaven was held by an astonishing 84 per cent of the sample. (Incidentally, as an admirable illustration of the new trend of retaining only the nice bits of religion, the corresponding percentage for a belief in the existence of hell was 53 per cent — hold on to heaven but abandon that whole hell thing; you can't fault the logic. I have a suspicion that the Catholic Church in Ireland plays along with these double standards.) The reduction in belief in heaven since 1991 was only about 3 per cent. Similarly in 1998, 70.7 per cent believed in the existence of religious miracles. This was only down about 3 per cent from 1991. So while the backbone or difficult parts of Catholicism — the rule adherence, prayer, attending mass, respect for Church authority — are declining fast, especially among the young, other aspects have stayed firm. These aspects are probably best described as mystical, magical ones — miracles and an everlasting heaven, and perhaps the perceived power of the "relics" or bones of saints — which have more in common with a pagan primitivism than Catholic Thomism. Interestingly, they are not at odds with a rising New Age mysticism and they do not contradict the claim that people will become more concerned with expressions of individual spirituality and idiosyncratic philosophy and less with unyielding doctrines.

Summing Up

The data show that Ireland has changed. What was once an utterly conservative country is now merely a conservative one. In comparative terms, the society must doubtless still rank as one of the most committed to God, but is no longer off the chart in comparison to other countries. In fact, it's beginning to look a little like other

Catholic countries such as Italy. This has consequences for church power. In the appendix to the later edition of his book, Inglis (1998) compares a sample of recent and older *Irish Times* headlines relating to the church. Reading them, one realises that where once the Catholic position on virtually every public issue was made known in no uncertain manner, now the hierarchy is far less forthright in putting across its opinion. Where the Church does make the news now, it is often in relation to scandals and the tone is naturally more apologetic than imperious. One might protest that it still has the numbers on its side — that even if the figures for weekly mass attendance are declining, there is nonetheless an impressive number of bums on seats come Sunday morning. But the strength in numbers is illusory. It may be an untapped psychological phenomenon, but to have the support of a declining 60 per cent of the population seems far weaker than, say, having a 40 per cent but growing share of public support. And as we've seen, most worrying for the church is that it is the youngest who are jumping ship fastest, so the rate of decline will, on current trends, accelerate. Even those who are still nominally loyal to the church are changing their values and are less comfortable with the dogmatic style of old — hence the decisive if narrow defeat of the anti-divorce forces in 1995. The church leadership has kept its powder remarkably dry since that defeat — they may live to fight another day but never again are likely to have the same influence, to have what amounted to a veto on government. The pattern of value change is likely to continue. And those who retain what might loosely be called metaphysical beliefs are more likely to think of spirituality, not religiosity, as the new black. It is more probable that they will search for expressions of this spirituality through flirtation with alternative and perhaps New Age belief systems. The old interchangeability or shorthand equation of Irish and Catholic is no longer valid. Strict Catholicism is a characteristic of the Old, not the New Irish Psyche.

Chapter 6

"SEX BEGAN IN 1993"

It was Philip Larkin, the poet, who wrote that "sexual intercourse began in nineteen sixty-three".[1] He was not (one assumes) suggesting that human sexual reproduction was unknown before that year but that a sea-change in attitudes had occurred in British society around this time. These were associated with new cultural, legal and technological innovations such as the contraceptive pill, the Beatles, the Penguin/Lady Chatterley trial, the mini-skirt, early hints of women's "lib" and so on. While human anatomy and biology stayed constant, sexual behaviour changed. British values and beliefs about sex underwent a complete transformation. Anyone who has read *The L-Shaped Room* and its description of the shame of single motherhood in 1950s London will appreciate the differences between then and now. One hesitates to apply the term "permissive", given its pejorative usage by small-minded conservatives, but certainly most Western societies have become more tolerant of alternative sexual expression.

Sexual intercourse did not literally begin in 1963 (although I believe the writer Martin Amis has claimed that oral sex evolved from a minority activity to the mainstream around then) but the swinging sixties undoubtedly changed the way people thought about it. And talked about it: for example, could even the sharpest trend-spotter from the 1970s have imagined phenomena like confessional daytime TV programmes, the outrageous double entendres of high-camp comedians, or women's magazines prominently devoting large numbers

---

[1] In "Annus Mirabilis".

of articles to sexual technique (unless it was "Knit Yourself an Or-gasm Today!")?

The process of post-materialisation should produce precisely this type of change, Ronald Inglehart has argued. The security of modern society and the easing of economic anxieties allow people to dissoci-ate sex from reproduction. Their interest in the exotic and tolerance of the new should create more openness to alternative sexual habits and lifestyles, for themselves and others. The decline of the authority of rule-bound religions and the increase in grey areas of morality (see previous chapter) loosen social constraints generally. Human sexual pleasure becomes a positive end in itself, something to be celebrated, not just a sordid by-product in the grim necessity of re-production.

No Sex Please — We're Irish

So how has Ireland fared? A popular book, *The Way We Live Now*, was published in 1996 by psychologist Dr Maureen Gaffney, based on her *Irish Times* articles published between the early to mid-1990s and dealt with various problems around relationships, adolescence and sexuality. One is struck with just how normal and sane it all is — apart from the articles on the "crisis of sexuality in the Catholic Church" and Irish emigration, this book could be offered as an ad-vice manual in any society. We learn that "feelings are the key" (p. 182), that "it is not enough for a partner to be responsive" (p. 107) and that most women "had faked orgasms at some time in their marriage" (p. 119). Feelings, responsivity and orgasms (even faked ones) in Ireland? Surely some mistake?

What is jarring is the description of sane, mature relationships *à la* Gaffney with contrasting literary attempts to capture Irish modes of sexuality. The characters of John B. Keane, Patrick Kavanagh or John McGahern inhabit a different world, one where frustration, lecherousness, and unquenched lust dominate. In the mainly rural environments of the past that they describe, men's views of the women they desire are permeated with bitterness and backward-ness. The contrast between Gaffney and McGahern is a product of the rapid change between Ireland of the 1950s and indeed 1970s and

1980s, and the present day (although see Patrick McCabe's novels for a contemporary take on the twisted tension between modernity and traditionalism). As we shall see from the available data, Ireland was a very strange place as regards sexual attitudes and behaviour. Things have changed very rapidly so that while it remains a very conservative country with regard to sexuality, it has converged a good deal with other European countries. Thus, one might paraphrase Larkin to suggest that sex in Ireland began in 1993.

In fact, the evolution of sexual norms closely parallels the shift in religious norms. The overlap with religion is not surprising, since Irish sexual attitudes and behaviour cannot be understood without understanding the influence of the Catholic church. These days, the church talks the talk around sex in a fairly modern way — a wonderful positive gift from God, and all that. But this is about as convincing as a former despot extolling the virtues of democracy. The official church line in the past on sex was that it was dirty and shameful — chastity was the ideal, sexual relations — preferably rare — within marriage a rather poor second, and anything else was mortally sinful. The damaging legacy of this almost medieval ideology still survives today. (Another famous Philip Larkin line, "they fuck you up, your mum and dad",[2] might have been adapted for Ireland thus, "they fuck you up, those priests and nuns".) Recently, I observed a conversation between a number of "progressive-minded" Irish and Dutch young people — when the topic turned to sexual matters, the Dutch were at ease, open, and mature — the Irish blushed, looked at the ceiling, joked or changed the subject. They were clearly embarrassed and squeamish about having a serious adult conversation on the topic. Similarly, a colleague of mine noted how young Canadian males were more matter-of fact *and knowledgeable* about the biology of menstruation than young Irish *females* — they had been provided with abundant, detailed and candid information in school, Irish students much less so. Ignorance and bashfulness are not cute. Nor are they healthy. A report on health in *The Irish Times*[3] showed that Irish

---

[2] In "This Be the Verse"

[3] 18 June 2001

people are more knowledgeable about foot-and-mouth disease in animals than about sexually transmitted disease in humans. And in a survey, only 30 per cent of people with sexual health problems said they would report them to their GP because of embarrassment.

But things are better and freer than they were in the past in Ireland. The introduction of the right to remarry is one example of this. Eurostat provides information on family life in Europe; in the Yearbook 2000 (p. 89), there are comparative data on divorce rates across the EU. The Irish data are missing, it appears at first glance. The footnote beneath the table of data reads, "Divorce not allowed before 1996". The starkness of the missing data and the authoritarianism of the message makes one study the figures again. Divorce "not allowed"? What country was that again? When did Iran join the EU? (Actually, that's a little unfair to Iran where divorces have always been relatively easy to obtain).

In what other ways did Ireland of the past stand apart from other European countries? Fertility rates of Irish women have been far higher than the European average. In Figure 6.1, the figures across the 15 (current) EU countries are presented for 1988.

Figure 6.1: Total Fertility Rate of EU Countries in 1988

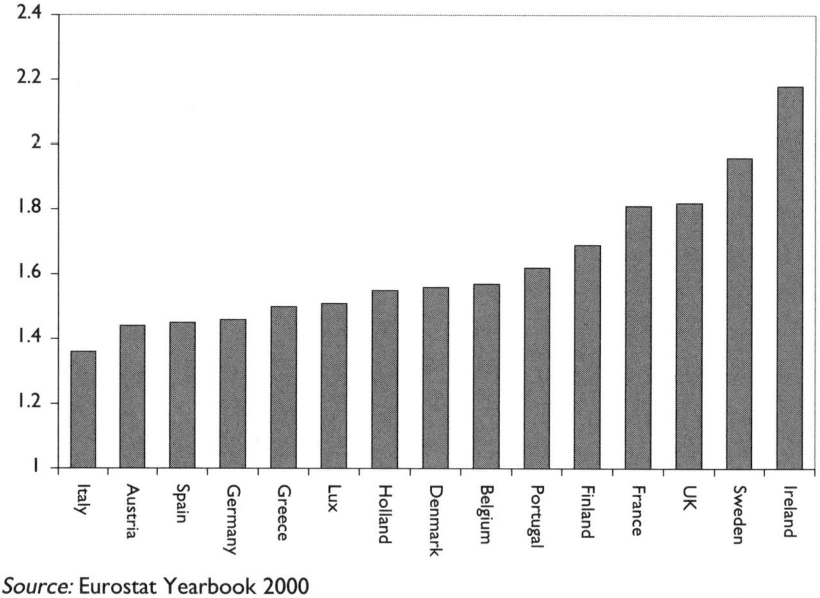

Source: Eurostat Yearbook 2000

Total fertility[4] was highest in Ireland, highlighting the trend towards large families that typified Ireland in the past. Completed fertility[5] for women born in 1950 in Ireland was three children compared to a European average of less than two. And Irish babies were more likely to be born within wedlock than the average European in 1988 — 88 per cent versus 82 per cent. The picture then of Ireland prior to the 1990s was a traditional one of large numbers of offspring born to married parents.

The New Climate

Things have changed, and very quickly. The former Taoiseach, Garret FitzGerald, has turned his attention to this aspect of Irish life in two shrewd opinion articles in *The Irish Times*, in 1997 and 2000. He commented:

> . . . both in their magnitude and in the speed at which they have been happening, the demographic changes that have been taking place . . . are dramatic. (*Irish Times*, 11 November 2000)

He summarised the new elements of Irish demography:

> . . . a very disturbing picture indeed emerges . . .: the decline in, as well as postponement of, marriage; the large and accelerating increase in marriage breakdown, . . .; and the huge increase in non-marital pregnancies involving births to teenage mothers. (*Irish Times*, 13 December 1997)

He goes on to argue that

> . . . for very many people, the institution of marriage has simply lost much of its significance . . . [there is] a widespread dissociation of marriage and child-bearing.

---

[4] "Total fertility of a calendar year is the average number of children that would be born alive to a woman during her lifetime if she were to experience during her childbearing years the age-specific fertility rates of the respective period". Eurostat Yearbook 2000, p. 93.

[5] "Completed fertility is the ultimate average number of children born alive to women born in a particular year", ibid.

This is a big and important set of claims by the former Taoiseach. What evidence does he draw on to support it? In terms of fertility, there has been an obvious decline. As FitzGerald points out, the Irish birth rate has declined rapidly since 1980, despite the fact that the number of women of child-bearing age is a fifth higher now than then. Births should have increased by about 10,000 rather than declined by about 20,000. FitzGerald's analysis draws out a nice statistical paradox in this regard. Fertility rates of Irish women appear to have increased if one looks at either marital or non-marital pregnancy groups. What has occurred simply is that fewer women are enjoying the pleasure of marriage or they are surviving longer without it. Since the marital birth rate is far greater than the non-marital, the net effect is an overall lowering of the number of childbirths. Overall, because fewer women are marrying, and those who do are marrying later, there is a decline in fertility.

Childbirth is becoming a matter of choice, rather than necessity and more women are choosing to put off motherhood until their thirties. The average age of within-marriage mothers in Ireland in 1980 was just over 29. By 1998, it was just over 32. The corresponding ages for mothers outside marriage was 22 in 1980 and 25 in 1998. The teenage unmarried mother phenomenon is declining in relative salience while non-marital births have increased. The firm association between parenthood and marriage is also loosening. Just over a decade ago, as noted above, the percentage of live births outside marriage was well below the EU average. By the end of the decade, the Irish rate was (marginally) ahead. The change in the two rates is represented in Figure 6.2.

Figure 6.2: Live Births outside Marriage as % of all Live Births

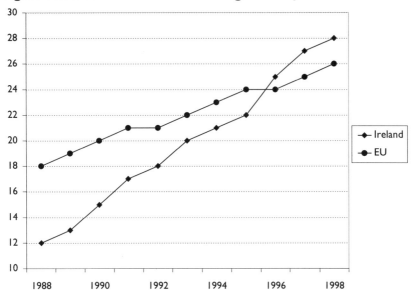

Note: the figure for the EU average in 1998 is based on the mean of available data. *Source:* Eurostat Yearbook 2000.

As Figure 6.2 shows, the trend towards the unlocking of parenthood and marital status was a broad European one. However, in Ireland the change was taking place far more quickly than elsewhere — at an electrifying pace, sociologically speaking. The increase in Ireland in that 11-year period of about 150 per cent was unmatched elsewhere (for example, the Dutch change was 120 per cent, the Greek was 100 per cent, the UK about 60 per cent, the Danes were unchanged).

FitzGerald's claims are thus built on firm foundations. Marriage has lost much of its social importance. It is no longer a normative prerequisite of parenthood, as we have noted. And while most people do still become legally married eventually, it is certainly in decline. Unmarried women can now be fun singletons, not withered spinsters. (The stigma was never so sharp for "bachelors".) The most recent censuses, taken in 1981, 1986, 1991 and 1996, show the increase in the proportion of those single in the 30–34 year old group. For males, the percentages were, respectively, 24 per cent, 26 per cent, 29 per cent and 37 per cent. For females, the corresponding percentages were 15 per cent, 17 per cent, 20 per cent and 27 per cent. The largest increase has therefore been between 1991 and 1996. The upcoming census (2002) has been delayed because of the foot-and-mouth crisis but is likely to show these trends increasing. The institution of marriage is also under attack from increasing levels of marital breakdown. In the last two divorce referenda, the no divorce groups argued, with perfectly straight faces, that divorce *causes* marriage breakdown. But the trends towards greater levels of marriage breakdown were already visible in the "separation" statistics. Divorce was not introduced until 1996 but by that year, there were 87,800 people separated compared with 55,100 in 1991 and 37,200 in 1986. This change, in the pre-divorce era, was phenomenal.

> The Census report [of 1996] shows that the greatest growth occurred in the categories "legally separated" and "other separated" each of which more than doubled between 1991 and 1996. (CSO press release)

FitzGerald has demonstrated that the rapid rate of increase is predictable from the age profiles — each younger generation in the census data shows far greater levels of marital breakdown than its same-age cohort in the previous census. In February 2000, Carol Coulter reported that divorce proceedings were also increasing rapidly in the late 1990s while the number of legal separations had not diminished, perhaps surprisingly given the availability of divorce (*Irish Times*, 28 February 2000).

The trend overall in Ireland is one where people feel less obliged to get married, are marrying later, no longer rigorously associate marriage and parenthood, or for that matter, see marriage as a strict precondition for having a sex life. And they are less willing simply to endure a married relationship that no longer meets their expectations.

O Tempora! O Mores!

But let's not get carried away. Up to the very recent past, Ireland has had a hardline conservativeness on sexual matters that stopped only just short of fundamentalism. Attitudes towards any "set-up" outside of the married heterosexual couple, industriously and joylessly reproducing devout offspring, were absolutely hostile. In 1991, the ISSP survey series asked respondents from a small number of countries their views on aspects of sexuality. The Irish were consistently the most traditional of the EU countries. Figure 6.3 displays the views of the samples on the wrongfulness of sexual relations either between same-sex adults or between a married person and someone who is not his/her spouse. The percentages in Figure 6.3 are those believing that these relations are *always* wrong.

Figure 6.3: Percentages Believing that Same-sex and Extra-marital Sexual Relations are Always Wrong

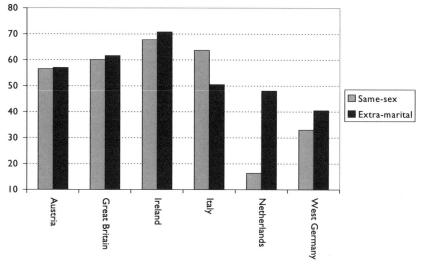

Source: ISSP 1991

Ireland is the leading conservative country, although the liberal Dutch in fact look more out of kilter given the surprisingly high level of opposition to homosexuality in many countries.

Access to abortion/termination was another source of troubled dispute in Ireland for much of the last two decades of the twentieth century and views on legalisation were very much in the minority. In the ISSP 1994 survey, for example, 28 per cent of Irish respondents agreed that abortion should be legal compared to 43 per cent of an Italian sample, 52 per cent from Great Britain, 53 per cent of a Dutch group and 89 per cent of those sampled in former East Germany. Eight of the current EU countries (including Ireland) were surveyed in the ISSP sweep of 1994. Figure 6.4 contrasts the Irish levels of agreement with the mean of the other seven (Austria, Germany, Italy, Netherlands, Spain, Sweden and the UK) towards the following survey items: couples can live together without getting married ("live together"); divorce is the best solution when a married couple can't work out their problems ("divorce solution"); sex before marriage is always wrong ("sex before marriage"); sexual relations between two consenting under-16-year-olds are always wrong (underage sex); and sexual relations between two same-sex adults are always wrong (gay sex).

Figure 6.4: Percentages of Irish and European Grouping of Respondents Expressing Strong Agreement on Five Survey Items

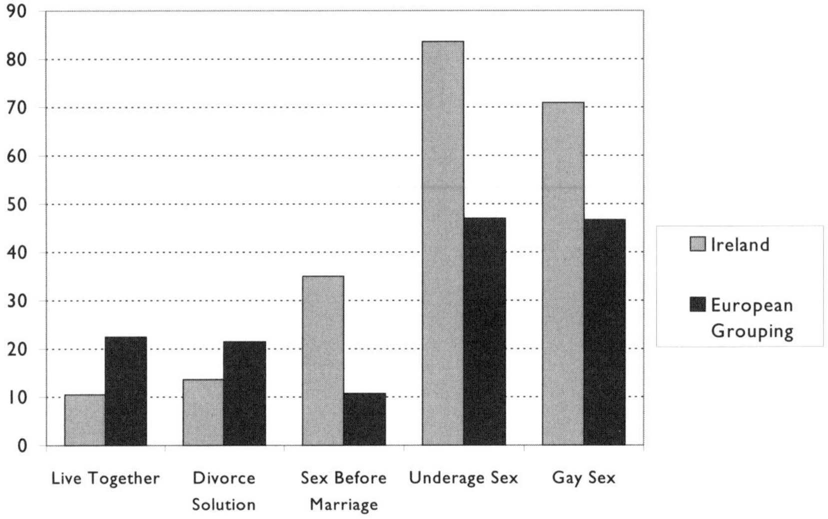

Source: ISSP 1994

Irish respondents were clearly and consistently more traditionalist across all items. Furthermore, the survey also picked up interesting differences on the ideal number of children for a family to have. Only 32 per cent of Irish respondents in 1994 felt that two or less was ideal while 70 per cent of the EU grouping opted for that range.

At the beginning of the chapter, shifts in marriage and reproductive *behaviour* were noted. Similarly conservative attitudes with regard to sex and reproduction, outlined above, have also altered rapidly. (Attitudinal change around sexuality undoubtedly creates the setting in which new forms of sexual behaviour may occur. And then of course, the existence and acceptance of new forms of behaviour implies and influences a further change in attitudes.) The trends have been in the direction of greater ambiguity about, or tolerance to-wards human relationships. There is an increasing recognition that one size may not fit all, the one size referring to the married hetero-sexual norm. That Ireland's attitudes are in transition as regards this domain is nicely picked up in the ISSP surveys 1991–1998 where three questions were replicated and so allow for comparison. The first is an item on the wrongfulness of sexual relations of a married person with someone other than his/her spouse. The percentages believing it to be always wrong in 1991 and 1998 are displayed in Figure 6.5 (left columns). For the purpose of comparison, the views of the samples of other EU countries as an average have been in-cluded.

Figure 6.5: Percentage of Respondents, Ireland and EU Grouping, Agreeing that Sex with other than Spouse (SOS), Premarital Sex (PS) and Gay Sex (GS) are Always Wrong

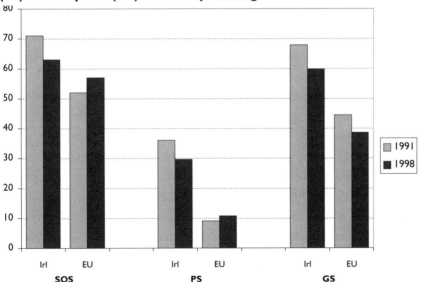

Source: ISSP 1991 and 1998

Clearly, in Figure 6.5, there is some evidence for convergence of views here. The most important point, though, is the change of view in Ireland. Note that the survey question does not necessarily imply deceitfulness — for example, the extra-marital relations might be consensual, an agreed part of an "open" relationship, or it might be the case that medical, physical or psychological problems have made sex impossible or unpleasant for one partner. The hardline position that these exceptions do not matter, or do not exist and that they are "always" wrong is held by a smaller majority in 1998.

On sexual relations before marriage, a similar pattern emerges. In Figure 6.5 (central columns), the change in views in this regard are clear. Again, there is some moderate evidence of a trend towards convergence across Europe. But the change of note is in Ireland, where less than three in ten believe now that sex before marriage is always wrong. This is significant given the anecdotal claims that a lot of Irish parents manage to live in denial about their sons' and (especially) daughters' lifestyle. Despite the mountain of evidence that she is living in London or Dublin with a partner, they stick rigidly to their moral code. Only when they telephone her at 5.00 a.m. with some urgent news and find themselves speaking to the "just a good friend" do they run out of delusional hiding places. It is then that serious thought about the nature of modern relationships is required. The survey data suggest that this serious thought now seems to be having an effect.

Also on the move are attitudes to gay relationships or rather gay sex. The distinction is not necessarily trivial. In an article in *The Observer*, the journalist Barbara Ellen has claimed that many people are quite tolerant of gay culture and relationships so long as they appear camp and sexless (*Life* supplement, 24 June 2001). It is the thought of people actually having gay sex that offends so many ("hate the sin, not the sinner" is the abbreviated church view). The ISSP survey is refreshingly direct in this regard and asks people their views on sexual relations between same sex people — the results are displayed in Figure 6.5 (right columns). There is evidence for a growing European-wide liberalism towards gay sex although the Irish position, even after some substantial change, is still very conservative in this area.

Nonetheless, the evidence is clear and consistent from these three items that attitudes towards sexual relations, in the very short space of time of seven years, have moved sharply towards a more liberal position. There is also some modest evidence of gender, class and age differences in rates of attitudinal change — these will be examined in greater detail in Chapters 10 and 11.

The Legal Structure

Legal and political life in Ireland in the 1990s has not failed to reflect change and increased tolerance. The referendum on divorce held in late 1995 led to the introduction of the right to remarry in Ireland in 1996, despite the opposition of conservative opinion. While the current Taoiseach has not availed of the new right to a divorce, it is not insignificant that he is open about living with his partner. In the past, this would not have been acceptable to the majority of the population. As it is, opposition to his current situation has to be coded in terms of awkwardness or inappropriateness and certainly, nobody would think to call for his resignation on these grounds.

Homosexuality has also been decriminalised since 1993, although had such a decision been brought before the people in a referendum then, it is hard to imagine it would have been passed. Discrimination, explicit and subtle, against gay men and lesbians, is still rampant and Ireland certainly must be one of the most difficult European societies in which to come out or live an openly gay life. But while ghettoisation continues, at least the ghetto has become a little larger and more varied. The derisory non-custodial sentences given to the Fairview Park killers of an allegedly gay man is a thing of the past and outright homophobia has declined somewhat. In December 2000, it was reported that there were now three gay bars in Dublin as well as 12 clubs that have one gay night per week. Cork has two such clubs, as does Limerick, while Galway has one. A number of gay B&Bs have also opened up throughout the country. The existence of these venues has been met with tolerance, or at least indifference, by most of the straight population, something difficult to imagine in the 1970s and 1980s. In terms of legislation, a journalist reviewing the situation claimed, on the basis of a discussion with activists, that

> . . . less than a decade after the decriminalisation of homosex-
> ual acts, this State has more comprehensive anti-
> discrimination protection for homosexuals than most of our
> EU partners. (Denis Staunton, *Irish Times*, 1 February 2000)

Contraception was once perceived as a deeply moral issue.
Haughey's "Irish solution to an Irish problem", the manner in which
he sought to make contraceptives only available through GPs to
married couples, reflected the concerns of an earlier age. I recall the
eminent Brian Farrell questioning a Minister for Justice on his plans
to put the condom machine in Trinity's Student Union building out
of action. Equally, I seem to remember a vaguely liberal politician on
TV in the early 1980s, vehemently denying that his proposals would
lead to "condoms on supermarket shelves, like in England". *Quel
horreur!* The last time I looked in to my local Tesco, they were
there on the shelf — with no audible outcry.

Legal abortion/termination remains unavailable in Ireland. The
proximity of British hospitals acts as an escape valve on demands for
legalisation. However, the X case was a step too much even for conservative Ireland and nobody (or rather only a small number) was
ultimately prepared to keep a teenager, pregnant through rape, in
Ireland against her wishes and those of her parents. Currently, the
Byzantine legal position is understood perhaps only by a small number of legal experts (possibly in disagreement with one another). The
public attitude overall remains opposed to "abortion on demand",
but the numbers prepared to accept a grey area of crisis pregnancies
where it could be allowed as well as those favouring outright availability are undoubtedly growing (see Chapter 11). The polemics that
arise from the proposed 25th amendment to the constitution in
2002 should reveal the increasingly nuanced outlook of the Irish
public towards abortion. While it will be a surprise if the pro-lifers
lose, the fact that concessions of principle have already been made
around "grey areas" like the use of the morning-after pill and the
IUD, and the prioritisation of the mother's life over that of the foe-
tus in some medical interventions, are revealing of change in themselves.

Let's Get Personal

The assessment of laws and attitudes are essential in understanding aspects of social change, but they tell us little about actual sexual practices and their evolution. Researchers cannot secretly observe bedroom habits of the public — although if they could, it would certainly galvanise interest in the study of social science. Voyeurism once removed is the best that can be achieved. One possibility is to interview a large sample of people about their sexual habits. The problems are, of course, the reluctance of people to tell the truth about intimate aspects of their lives, recruiting skilled interviewers who can ask these questions sensitively, and of course, the cost of such an enterprise.

In the absence of such data, one substitute is to look at the "personal" section of the small ads. *Buy and Sell* is the biggest-selling free ads magazine in Ireland. Volumes from mid-June were examined in 1991, 1996 and 2001, i.e. at three points over a ten-year period. In 1991, there were no ads of a personal nature, except for two middle-aged American males in the Pen Pals section, promising to write back to all who wrote, bless them. By 1996, there were two sections for "people looking for people", one via voicemail and one via box number. By 2001, there were five distinct sections — women looking for men, men looking for women, women looking for women, men looking for men and alternative lifestyles. Using these categories as an admittedly flimsy measure, we can get some sense of the increase in sexual interest and diversity among a section of the Irish population. (Incidentally, it may be protested that in relying on figures provided by a commercial magazine, one learns more about magazine policy than public taste. I disagree — even if such figures do represent a direct change in editorial policy, that change in policy in turn is based on beliefs about acceptability of certain advertisements as well as public demand.) Figure 6.6 compares the number of ads over the three time periods.

Figure 6.6: Number of Personal Ads by Type Appearing in **Buy and Sell***, mid-June, 1991, 1996, 2001*

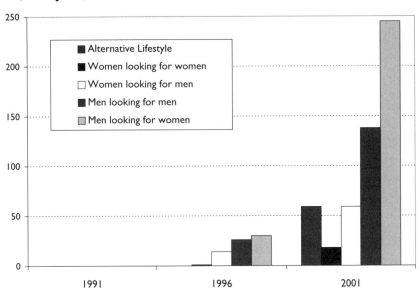

The headings are self-explanatory in Figure 6.6, apart from "alternative lifestyle". This section represents an explicit break with the norm of dichotomous human sexual relations, since virtually all the ads deal with "three or moresomes" — individuals (mainly male) looking for couples, couples looking for individuals (mainly female), or couples looking for couples. An example of the last case is the following ad: "Professional couple, late 30s, both very adventurous and broad-minded wltm like-minded couples for fun. Can travel." (Toto, I have a feeling we're not in Kansas anymore).

Nineties Ireland also witnessed the acceptance of sexual pleasure as a purchasable commodity. That is of course not to say that one could not purchase sex before that — Joyce's *Ulysses* provides ample detail of such transactions near the turn of the last century. But social norms around the *acceptability* of its commercialisation have changed. The decision by the authorities not to prosecute the sale of adult men's magazines means that even humble grocery franchises have become purveyors of explicit pornography. No doubt that decision was in part motivated by the difficulty of censoring the Internet, but it also reflected greater public tolerance on the issue. Adult shops catering to exotic tastes have opened up in many cities and towns. The Golden Pages for Dublin, for example now lists 12 of these shops in Dublin with display adverts offering, *inter alia*, videos, erotic lingerie, latex, leatherware, boots and shoes, creams and adult toys. A substantial sex shop on one of the major thoroughfares of the capital would have been unthinkable in 1980s Ireland — a time when the Monty Python film, *The Meaning of Life*, was banned because of its mocking (but catchy) number, "Every Sperm is Sacred". And the new vogue for lap-dancing clubs means that while his wife is at her weekly bridge session, the middle-aged man, driven demented by the juxtaposition of the words "scantily" and "clad", can get to see nubile young women strut their stuff. Comely maidens lap-dancing at the crossroads? Dev must be turning in his grave.

You've Come a Long Way Baby

Today's Ireland is unrecognisable in relation to sexuality in comparison to even the recent past of 10 or 15 years ago. In this regard, the past is indubitably another country. That we still remain one of the most conservative societies in Europe tells us a lot about the extreme and bizarre society that existed previously. It was Catholic guilt and body-hatred *par excellence*. This guilt has not been entirely absolved and attitudes, behaviour and laws are still marked by the past. But while now we find our values on the conservative end of the scale, at least we're *on* the scale, not some freak outlier off the map (there are close similarities to religious change in this regard). While other countries like the UK or the Netherlands show stability with regard to sexuality, change continues at a dramatic pace in Ireland. This journey will run and run, and many, especially traditionalists who remember how it all used to be, will find the ultimate destination very disturbing. There may even be recurring attempts to go back to where we were. But these sporadic attempts at backlash will fail. The quiet sexual revolution will not be rolled back.

Chapter 7

TWO DECADES ARE A VERY LONG TIME IN POLITICS

Or are they? How recognisable is the Irish political system from that which existed in the 1970s and 1980s? What sort of difference does it make if public debates take place now in a more secular environment and a once powerful actor on the political stage, the church, has been relegated to a minor role? Does a nation no longer gripped with fear of emigration and unemployment have the same priorities and demonstrate the same electoral practices as previously? One theory, mentioned in some of the previous chapters, has been offered by Ronald Inglehart. He proposes that an altered economic environment inevitably changes priorities, values and voting styles. The rise of Green parties and ecological movements as serious political players in most European countries, he attributes largely to the young and the fact that their maturation to adulthood coincided with an era of political certainties and economic abundance. The voice of protest, he suggests, switched away from the materialist forces of the past, such as the mass communist parties of western Europe and towards alternative anti-authoritarian, pro-equality movements like the New Left in the 1970s, anti-nuclearism of the 1980s and the anti-discrimination campaigns of the 1990s. Recently, I walked through Dublin on the Mayday holiday. I passed a radical Left/Green anti-globalisation demonstration and overheard a frustrated van driver. Stuck in a traffic jam because of this activity, he angrily denounced the "rich Greens out protesting". Doubtless, he and Inglehart both share the same underlying model of action — in order to feel an urgency about global fairness and democracy, one's basic material concerns must already be answered.

Does Ireland's evolution match the predictions that Inglehart has been brave enough to make? He has suggested that, as societies move from economic uncertainty to greater confidence, there should be a transition in their politics from "insecurity", characterised by a belief in the need for strong leaders, a demand for order and unquestioning obedience, and closed-minded xenophobic attitudes, to that of "security", characterised by a de-emphasis on political authority, a priority for individual self-expression, an interest in the novel and exotic, and a demand for active participation in political decision-making.

Ireland's politics in the past certainly could have done with some of the latter. A stultifying system has dominated since the Civil War cleaving of Sinn Féin. While the "national question" arguably still had a relevance to political debate (in many ways, it remains the "hottest" question), the division between Fianna Fáil and Fine Gael on this issue became ultimately barren since both shared the same formal line on the North. Difference existed only at the level of political rhetoric, nuance, and outlook of the membership. And this meant that other potentially real political differences were inevitably muffled. Thus, discourse and debate remained confused and immature at the national level. The failure of a mass social democratic party and class-based politics to develop and the role of the Labour Party only as a minor and occasional coalition partner were symptomatic of the quirkiness of the system. Some commentators have been correct to point out that the British political model was overused as the standard against which Ireland was compared, since Britain's monarchy and hereditary peerage, constitutionalism without a constitution and ultra-centralism were oddities themselves. Nonetheless, Ireland's system at times bore all the hallmarks of parochialism gone mad. Fianna Fáil developed as the party of consummate operators, the quintessential cute hoors, adept, even by the standards of the political classes, at talking out of both sides of their mouths. Fine Gael tried, with varying degrees of success, to match the clientelism, backscratching and nods'n'winks of their larger competitors. And how did the Irish people respond? They obediently lay back, closed their eyes and thought of (emigrating to) England.

Politically speaking, official Ireland is still represented by Fianna Fáil and Fine Gael, descendants of the two civil war parties. How have they survived into the new millennium? Quite well, it turns out. To a reasonable degree, these parties have been able to change with the times and maintain relevance for the majority of the Irish people. However, that success must not prevent us from seeing another, slower pattern of decline in their popular vote. While voting in an election, once perhaps every four years, is an admittedly limited form of participation in the system, it remains one of the most important measures of opinion about politics (both in the decision taken to vote and the choice/s made). If one examines data on the percentage of the population voting in the last five general elections — November 1982, 1987, 1989, 1992, 1997 — the turnout in general elections, as opposed to the dismal showing in many referenda, has been fairly consistent and has drifted only about 2 per cent either side of 65 per cent. (This is calculated by assessing the number of votes cast nationally, divided by the population for each of these years as derived from the CSO's national population estimate, less one quarter to compensate, roughly, for under-18-year-olds.) While not very high by international standards, neither is it very low and there is no strong evidence of a growing and widespread disenchantment with parliamentary politics.

However, there is evidence of some growing disenchantment with certain parliamentary political parties. This becomes clear if the percentage votes for Fianna Fáil and Fine Gael are combined — as galling as the idea might be to many members of these rival parties — to generate a measure of overall public satisfaction with the political orthodoxy. The average of the combined percentage of their vote in the two elections in the 1990s was 65.4 per cent in comparison to three earlier 1980s elections, when it had been 75.4 per cent. The drop is over 10 per cent of the voting population — not a revolution by any means, but a significant shift, particularly if the trends were to continue in that direction (their combined vote in the local elections of June 1999 was 65.1 per cent). Applying the reasonable, if obvious, mathematical rule that votes cast for candidates other than Fianna Fáil and Fine Gael must make up the remainder of the 100 per cent, it suggests that smaller parties and independents have made inroads into the popularity of the two larger parties.

Political Value Change — Some Positive Signs

Voting patterns may be an important but sometimes crude barometer of change. What evidence emerges from more routine surveying of opinions? There are some signs of fundamental shifts in value priorities. Inglehart has argued that the resolution of material concerns permits the emergence of values that may be more "post-materialist". The Eurobarometer surveys allow individuals to select two options from a list of four to represent their priorities. An example of a materialist priority is "fighting rising prices" while "ensuring people have more say in their work and community" is a post-materialist one. Figure 7.1a presents the ratio of materialist items picked in comparison to post-materialist ones for Ireland and for the rest of the EU. Higher scores indicate a greater predominance of materialist priorities. The three time periods are surveys gathered from 1973 to 1979, from 1980 to 1989 and from 1990 to 1992.

Figure 7.1a: Proportion of Materialist to Post-materialist Responses, Ireland and EU, 1970s, 1980s and early 1990s

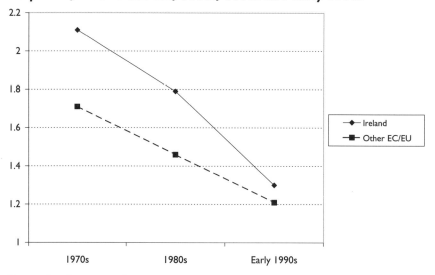

Source: Eurobarometer Surveys

The steady increase in the proportion of post-materialist responses into the early 1990s is visible. And while the rest of the EU was steadily growing more "post-materialist", Ireland was catching up fast. In other respects, there were increasing signs of growing passion and awareness among the public. As a measure to tap political interest, respondents were asked (again in Eurobarometer) whether they tried to engage friends on political issues, with responses ranging from "never" to "often". The authors of the Eurobarometer also constructed a scale as a combined measure of several different questions relating to political interest — this they call "cognitive mobilisation" (high mobilisation indicates greater active interest in politics). Figure 7.2a below presents the aggregated data, again from three periods, and contrasts Ireland with the rest of the EU. As the diagram shows, the direction of change is positive with a growing number of people interested in the political process in Ireland.

Figure 7.2a: Changes in Measures of Political Interest at Different Times, Ireland and the EU/EC

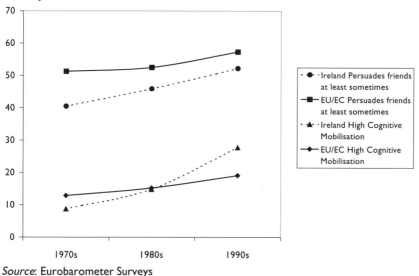

Source: Eurobarometer Surveys

Inglehart has suggested that the political styles of post-materialist or secure societies are increasingly characterised by rejection of authoritarianism, demands for increased participation and alternative expressions. The ISSP survey of 1996 examined the attitudes of a representative sample of citizens of 23 countries towards govern-ment and political activity. A majority of the Irish sample did appear to hold a number of anti-establishment views. For example, 60.2 per cent agreed that there were occasions when one should follow one's conscience and break the law (rather than obey the law without ex-ception). An overwhelming 84.3 per cent believed that public meet-ings to protest against the government should definitely or probably be allowed, while 78.8 per cent had the same tolerance of public demonstrations. And smaller majorities said that they personally would attend a public meeting (62.4 per cent) or a demonstration to protest a government decision (53.4 per cent).

Other Signs of a Healthy Body Politic . . .

In 1948, a group of researchers, sometimes called the "Berkeley school", and heavily influenced by psychoanalytic thinking, suggested that one of the principal components of an "Authoritarian Personality" was an inability by individuals to be critical of their own parents or indeed any power figure. In a not entirely dissimilar fashion, Inglehart has suggested that insecure societies are unable to accept criticism of the establishment while secure societies can cast a keenly appraising eye over their mis-rulers. Discontent with the establishment in Ireland surely took form and substance in a number of tribunals of inquiry. The least successful, by broad consensus, was the Beef Tribunal set up in May 1991 (see Fintan O'Toole's remorseless account of this epi-sode, published in 1995). However, in the latter part of the decade, parallel to our dizzying economic success, and after some initial scep-ticism, we were gleefully dragging the old establishment before us to answer for their behaviour — and perhaps surprising them with the vigour of the tribunals. Had any of the old political class been stupid enough (since they certainly had the arrogance in spades) to have erected statues to themselves, we would surely have toppled them.

The Flood Tribunal commenced its work in 1998 to examine pay-ments for land development. As a result, some senior figures have been drummed out of politics, smooth PR people have turned into trembling, green-faced wrecks in the witness stand and at the time of writing, one prison bunk has been capaciously, if briefly, filled. A year previously, the

McCracken Tribunal, set up on 7 February, examined the generous payments to Charles Haughey and Michael Lowry by Ben Dunne and uncovered Ansbacher accounts in the sunny Cayman Islands as well as opening a window on the way in which the Golden Circle in Ireland side-stepped onerous tax demands. This revelation led to the setting up of the Moriarty Tribunal, mainly to examine the manner in which Haughey was maintained by large payments from the rich. Because we are accustomed to it now, it is not as shocking as once it was, so it is worth pausing — this is Charlie Haughey we're talking about. Charles J. Haughey, The Squire. Not just *a* political leader from the 1980s but, in many ways, *the* leader. He liked to be called "The Boss", after all. At the time, even other senior political figures were terrified of him and happily tugged forelocks in his presence. And now we're probing through his accounts, we're costing his drinks cabinet and scanning his restaurant bills. For goodness sake, we even know his taste in shirts (expensive, natch). Ruffling through the dirty linen of the *Lidero Maximo* — does it get more anti-establishment than this? And other prominent politicians, medics, and academics have been called before us to explain the behaviour of the powerful towards haemophiliacs in the Lindsay Tribunal. So wealth has not made the nation complacent, it would seem, but sharper, more critical, more vigilant.

Meanwhile, the security and political stability prevailing here has also meant that a greater number of people want to come to live in this country than to leave it, historically a rare phenomenon. And some of those coming here are different in race, nationality and culture to the main populace. The post-materialist thesis proposes that a secure society should be more open to the novel, the exotic, to "otherness". Although the numbers and size of minority communities are small, the ethnic diversity of central Dublin, for example, has clearly and visibly grown. Recently, the British Psychological Society asked its members to provide it with their personal details — the categorisation of ethnicity meant that one could be an Irish psychologist or a black psychologist, but not both. The axiom that Irishness equals whiteness more or less held true (statistically speaking) up to the 1990s but it is clear that this will change, and indeed already has. The government has supported the creation of a National

Consultative Committee on Racism and Interculturalism as well as a media campaign to aid the integration of minorities into Irish society. Writers as intelligent as Declan Kiberd have argued that

> . . . the historical capacity of the Irish to assimilate waves of newcomers should never be underestimated . . . the Normans became more Irish than the Irish themselves. Who is to say that the latest group of arriving Nigerians might not know the same destiny? (An excerpt from his essay in *Multiculturalism: the View from the Two Irelands* published in *The Irish Times*, p. 3, Weekend Supplement, 19 May 2001)

He also argues that the racist element in the initial public outcry was "often broken down once first-hand relationships began".

One Step Forward, One Step Back: The Democratic Deficit (1)

But some strange things start happening when we look a little closer at Irish politics, some phenomena that make it more difficult to hail the progressive march of history. For example, on interrogating the survey data later in the 1990s, some of the trends change direction. Earlier in this chapter, in Figure 7.1a, the trend towards greater post-materialism in the 1970s, 1980s and early 1990s were displayed. However, in 7.1b below, the comparable figures for 1999 have been added.

Figure 7.1b: Materialism in Ireland and EU from the 1970s to 1999

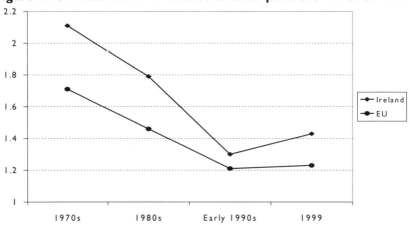

Source: Eurobarometer Surveys

The period of sharpest economic growth has *not* coincided with declining levels of materialism. In fact, while the EU levels have stabilised, there has been a slight increase in the recorded level of materialist priorities among the Irish sample. Similarly, if the data gathered most recently for a measure of political interest — i.e., trying to persuade friends at least sometimes about politics — are included, as in Figure 7.2b, another decline is apparent.

Figure 7.2b: One Measure of Political Interest in Ireland and the EU/EC, 1970s to 2000*

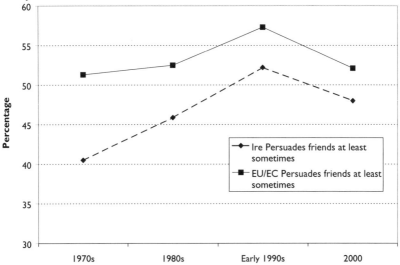

Note: * Core questions are replicated in some but not all Eurobarometers. The most recently available to the author are included in each piece of analysis.
Source: Eurobarometer Surveys

We may want to believe that a new generation of activists walks among us. That might indeed be the case, but if so, they are a small minority. For the bulk of the population, the 1990s were not a time of great political interest. At least according to the measure in Figure 7.2b, fewer Irish people felt inclined to be passionate or persuade others of their views at the end of that decade in comparison to the beginning. The disenchantment appears to be part of a general European trend.

Other measures paint a similar picture, whereby not only was there no explosion of participatory demands among Irish people in the 1990s, but the numbers of radical citizens actually diminished. The ISSP surveys, for example, showed that while 52 per cent of the Irish sample in 1990 thought that "organising public meetings to protest against the government" should definitely be allowed, by 1996, the corresponding percentage had actually declined to 48 per cent. And in 1996, 60 per cent of the Irish sample thought that one should follow one's conscience even if it meant breaking the law on occasion, while in 1990 the figure had been 63 per cent. The decline is not large, but the significance lies in the failure of a challenging postmaterialist politics to grow. In 1996, only 42 per cent believed that protest marches should definitely be allowed. Forty-two per cent? This falls short even of majority support. The comfortable acceptance of the status quo is also exposed in a telling figure — in 1996, the ISSP survey asked Irish respondents whether they had actually been on a protest demonstration or a public protest meeting in the previous five years — over 90 per cent had attended neither. This is a critical point — the abstract approval of a (bare) majority of the population for certain (basic) democratic rights is hardly the active engaged politics and political discourse of which silent revolutions are made.

As for the tribunals: as powerful as they have been in exposing the levels of routine corruption at the heart of the system, it is questionable whether they are a product of an enlightened public. Rather, a handful of intelligent journalists, determined judges and well-paid lawyers have done most of the digging. And they have been lucky. The downfall of this wayward wing of the elite has had more to do with their own hubris than a consequence of a nation intent on social justice and transparency. As Gene Kerrigan and Pat Brennan note in their book, *This Great Little Nation*, it was the material generated as a result of the Dunne family wars that acted as the spark to the majority of the tribunals. If Ben Dunne had not "freaked out" on cocaine on the seventeenth floor of a Florida hotel, there is a good chance that it may never have come to light. "The hotel employee who provided the nose candy for Ben Dunne probably hadn't a clue what he started" (Kerrigan and Brennan, 1999: 97), but may have done more for Irish democracy than most Irish citizens who knew something was amiss but refused to question too deeply. Similarly, payments to politicians like Ray Burke were exposed not by the vigilance of the people and their representatives, but by the corrupt James Gogarty whose greed and bitterness led him to fall out with his former employers at the JMSE building firm.

Racism and Vanity — The Democratic Deficit (2)

Despite wishful thinking, Ireland's financial success has not led to a generosity of spirit and tolerance towards ethnic minorities or an appreciation of the exotic or new. As a culture, the exclusivity of the very concept of Irishness has historically been exposed both in its partial refusal to recognise members of religious minorities such as Jews and Anglicans as "truly" Irish, as well as the unashamed and al-most universal denigration, abuse and mockery of the Travelling community. Nor is there much evidence in the last decade that new minorities in Ireland have been welcomed at a national level; the best that they can hope for is a suspicious begrudging acceptance, while the worst . . . ? The worst reaction has been enough, as an Irish col-league of mine working in the UK commented, to make the suburbs of south London (where the black teenager Stephen Lawrence was murdered by racists) look like a haven of inter-racial harmony. In May 2001, the website of Amnesty International (Ireland) contained a section called the "reality of racism" in Ireland in which sickening accounts of verbal and physical abuse towards minorities are pro-vided. Data gathered both by the African Refugee Network as well as by myself and Sinead Casey (2000) among minority groups in Ire-land show that the experience of abuse is typical, not exceptional. In defence, it might be argued that it only takes a relatively small num-ber of determined people to make the lives of minorities hellish. But again, survey work funded by Amnesty as well as non-partisan aca-demic work (see Curry, 2000) confirms that large chunks of the Irish population are deeply hostile to contact of any sort with all "outsid-ers", including foreigners, ethnic or national minorities, etc.

Despite the prevalence of felt and expressed hostility towards minorities, the 1995 ISSP survey of 11 countries (not including for-mer Eastern bloc countries), showed that an Irish sample had the highest level of pride in the "fair and equal treatment of all groups in society" (e.g. 21 per cent of the Irish sample were "very proud", compared to 18 per cent of Americans, 15 per cent of British, 13 per cent of Dutch and 7 per cent of German respondents). This corresponds with measures of pride generally, where inevitably Irish respondents show far higher levels than elsewhere. For example, in the Eurobarometer data based on EU countries (1997), 44 per cent of the EU-wide sample (bar Ireland) were very proud of their own country. This contrasts with 78 per cent of Irish respondents, who reported themselves being very proud of Ireland. Asked about pride in the history of their country, again Irish respondents were most self-regarding, with 53 per cent stating that they were very proud compared to 49 per cent of Americans, 39 per cent of Italians, 23 per cent of Norwegians, and 8 per cent of Germans (ISSP, 1995). This pride and the absence of national self-criticism (or even the ability for self-criticism) are pervasive but largely unremarked-upon aspects of Irish society. Yet they underpin an obsession with ourselves as a topic of discussion, our desperation for praise from foreigners, and also to a large extent, our failure to empathise with the plight of people from elsewhere except in the most self-aggrandising, tokenistic or patronising way.

Unequal Opportunities — The Democratic Deficit (3)

Irish society also remains deeply unequal in terms of power but especially of wealth. The US Central Intelligence Agency makes it its business to dig out information about every country in the world. In their annual Factbook, they even make public some of this intelligence information. One measure they try to obtain for countries is their degree of economic (in)equality. A standard way to do this is to compare the proportion of wealth of the poorest 10 per cent of the population with the richest 10 per cent. This measure is sometimes referred to as the Gini coefficient. Higher scores are an indication of greater inequality — for example, a Gini coefficient of 20 means that the top 10 per cent of the population have 20 times the wealth of the bottom 10 per cent. The CIA World Factbook 2000[1] provides the latest available data for ten EU countries (but not unfortunately for Austria, Germany, Luxembourg, Portugal and Greece). The scores are presented diagrammatically in Figure 7.3. The accuracy of these measures was confirmed by the more recent publication of the UN report on Human Development (2001) — of 17 selected (wealthiest) OECD countries, Ireland ranked second in terms of the proportion of people living in poverty and was sandwiched between the UK in third place and the US in first (p. 152).

Figure 7.3: Inequality Measures in Ten EU Countries

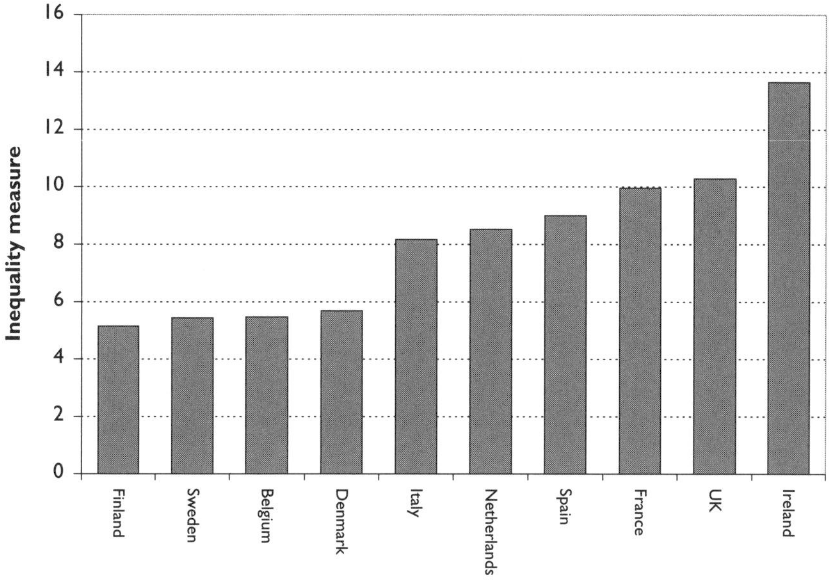

Source: CIA World Factbook 2000

Figure 7.3 tells its own tales (for example, that the top 10 per cent in Ireland own proportionally almost three times more of their economy than equivalent groups in Finland or Sweden) but also poses the question — with this measure of inequality, why aren't we a country of determined socialists? A partial answer is that for various complex reasons, free-market, *laissez-faire* thinking (in economics anyway) has not been strongly contested in Ireland. Evidence for this is provided

[1] See http://cia.gov/cia/publications/factbook

in the 1996 ISSP survey on the role of government. Often surveys make the mistake of asking if people agree with various positive-sounding goals and find that large majorities do. But the ISSP 1996 survey was excellently worded, since it asked people to make a choice between "reducing taxes" *or* "spending more on social services". An overwhelming 68 per cent of the Irish sample selected a reduction in taxation as their preferred choice.[2] Of 26 countries[3] sampled, only three had higher proportions opting for a reduction in taxation. And elsewhere, in the biannual Eurobarometer survey, assessments of respondents' self-rating on a left–right scale almost universally produce a disproportionally low percentage of Irish leftists compared to other EU countries.

The reality is that, while Irish politics has changed in many ways over the last two decades (policy questions, leading figures, the sophistication of discourse), the suspicion that most Irish have of all types of political ideology, especially of a leftish nature — as inherently wrong and "a bit foreign" — has not diminished. While the modest decline in the electoral support of the two largest parties was noted earlier in this chapter, perhaps the more important aspect of voting patterns has been the failure of any openly ideological party to grow in any significant way. Whether the ideology is ecological (the Green Party), explicitly Thatcherite (the PDs), nationalist (Sinn Féin), or leftist (the Labour Party, Socialist Party, Workers Party, Socialist Workers Party, the Communist Party or the defunct Democratic Left), it hasn't sold well on the doorsteps and in polling centres. And it's not an accidental phenomenon. To have one large, centre-right political party may be considered a misfortune; to have two looks like wilfulness.

---

[2] In an Irish Times/MRBI survey on 5 June 2001, of a sample of Irish respondents, 74 per cent were willing to forego further tax cuts in order to improve the health service. Aside from the fact that substantial tax cuts had already been enjoyed, this result says more about the perilous state of the health service (see Chapter 8) and its negative publicity than revealing a fundamental shift in ideology.

[3] "Jurisdictions" is in fact more accurate than "countries", since for example Germany was recorded as two areas for this question (former east and west).

One of the principal conceits of Irish political values is that we are "part of Europe". It's certainly true that at one level the Irish remain among the most enthusiastic pro-EU countries. The Eurobarometer (53) 2000 survey showed that the Irish were most likely to agree that EU membership is a good thing (76.4 per cent compared, for example, to 75.5 per cent of Luxembourgers, an EU average of 51 per cent and 25.2 per cent of a UK sample). Furthermore, 66 per cent of Irish respondents felt that the EU conjured up a very or fairly positive image compared to 41 per cent for the rest of the EU. But knowledge has not caught up with attitude. In 1998, the Eurobarometer survey asked people to name the forthcoming common European currency. The percentage correctly identifying the "euro" in each country is displayed in Figure 7.4.

Figure 7.4: Percentage Correctly Identifying the "Euro"

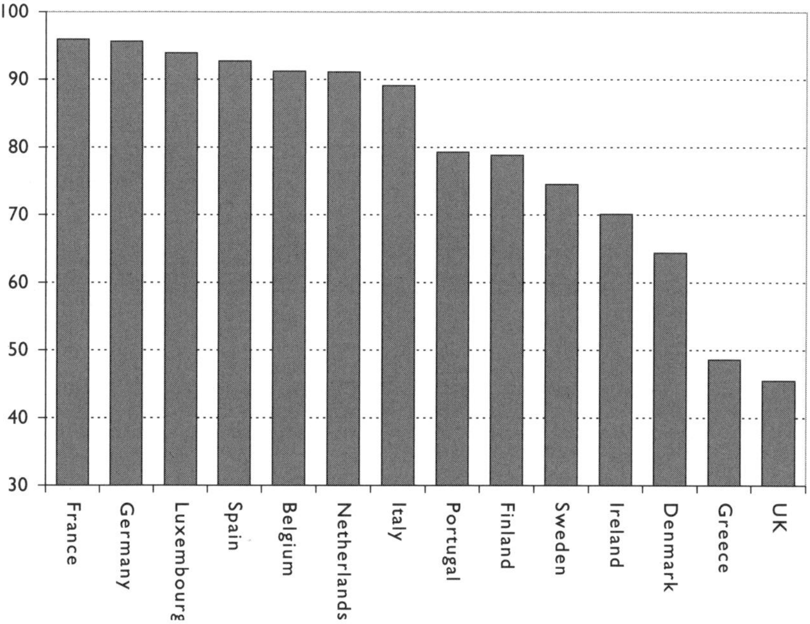

Source: Eurobarometer 50

As Figure 7.4 shows, Ireland is not at the bottom of the class, but at least the three nations scoring lower, the Greeks, British and Danes, had a good excuse — they did not participate in the first wave of entry to the common European currency.[4] Ireland did. The figures sum up the Irish stance on the EU perfectly — some enthusiasm but only the haziest knowledge of where, what, or how the Union operates. Fervent Europhilia is not an expression of Ireland's internationalism, except perhaps among a gaggle of creepy Young Fine Gaelers. Rather, the enthusiasm is a function of self-serving appetites — for most Irish people, "Brussels" is a set of 1970s buildings, set somewhere west of *mitteleuropa*, inhabited by efficient Germans, fun-loving but corrupt Mediterraneans, and kindly Belgians. We have tended to like "Brussels" because it gave us money to build roads and factories and fund hedge payments and heifers and such like. In return, in the past, all we had to do was to fly the European flag in a few prominent places, make vaguely liberal noises about the rights of women and gays, and try to show some discretion in the cronies we selected for the juicy jobs on offer there.

Thus, our Europeanness is mainly a product of selfishness, delusion and wishful thinking while its internationalist aspect is at best superficial. The Nice Treaty vote of June 2001 reflected this very accurately. The percentages were 16 per cent in favour, 18 per cent against and 66 per cent don't care (abstainers and spoiled votes). Why bother turning out when the vote has no discernible short- to medium-term advantage for Ireland? Why make the effort of finding out about a complex treaty if it's ultimately to benefit poorer Eastern European economies (and thereby threaten Ireland's poor mouth role at Brussels)? And while a certain sly anti-foreignerism played a role in the vote, as did a rump hardline Christian right ethos, a general public attitude of self-centredness was the main factor. This attitude has an occasional skin-deep European internationalism but is more profoundly driven with an instinctive "what's in it for us?" component.

Although it is not a popular claim, Ireland's politics in fact bear closer resemblance to those of the US than of continental Europe. In Figure 7.3, the relatively very high levels of social inequality obtaining in Ireland were displayed — had the US been included, the Irish Gini coefficient would have been most proximate to its score of 19. Similarly,

---

[4] Greece did not initially meet the criteria set out in the Maastricht Treaty.

typical of both societies are strong hostility to cosmopolitan ideology, the historical absence of a mass social-democratic party and extreme national self-centredness. The political style of each is principally characterised by PCP — Parochialism, Clientelism and above all, Pragmatism.

Conclusions

That Irish politics have changed in the last decades is not in question. The modest decline in support of the major two parties has been identified. Similarly, the presence of issues that are of at least some concern now — for example, related to the environment and ethnic minorities — did not and perhaps could not have existed previously. The language of debate has also changed. No one, for instance, is likely to engage in a bout of Jew-baiting in a Dáil speech as the late and largely unlamented Oliver J. Flanagan once did. Even "jokey" sexist references to the role of women have become rare. Anti-Traveller comments are more likely to emanate from local councillors than national representatives. In all, the discourse is more civilised or at least polished. And corrupt practices are no longer flaunted in the faces of the little people who pay the taxes.

Irish politics are not the same as they were 20 years ago. But it is difficult to say they are any better, and certain odious elements of the system remain intact. Voters do not appear to have transformed themselves *en masse* into a new post-materialist generation, an active demanding citizenry. Protest activity and radical participation have not, as yet, become anything like the norm, or even the norm for a significant minority. The small but significant national and ethnic minorities appearing in Irish towns and cities from elsewhere have stirred discussion and sometimes hostility but still little empathy or thinking on the meaning of Irish identity. One suspects that political correctness is quite widely understood and shrewdly used, rather than having changed public thinking at a profound level.

The Green Party has become a substantial conduit for protest votes but has not been accepted as a party worthy of power (hence its proportionally greater success in the elections perceived as less important, such as those for the European Parliament). Its problem, as noted earlier, and the problem of the smaller parties, is that they get serious about principle and ideology, a habit so alien to the Irish system. The only exception is the reverence given to the principle of parochialism, "my area first", to such a degree that regional prejudices often outweigh party political ones. And, naturally, nationalist self-interest overwhelms internationalist or European idealism. Thus, alongside the universal phenomenon of Nimbyism — Not In My Back Yard — which makes, for example, a coherent waste disposal policy impossible to create, Ireland also excels in Dimbyism (Definitely In My Back Yard) for anything worthwhile, e.g. new factories and wide roads. The short-sightedness and self-centredness of Irish politics have had implications for government spending and it is to this topic that we turn in Chapter 8.

Chapter Eight

THE GROWTH DIVIDEND: WHERE DID ALL THE MONEY GO?

When the Soviet Union disintegrated, the balance of world politics and military affairs was profoundly altered. It was expected, or at least hoped, that the ending of the sometimes cold, sometimes warmish, war between the two superpowers that had characterised most of the late twentieth century might yield some positive benefits. For example, the huge proportion of GNP that the USA and (unsustainably) the USSR had previously invested in military resources might be used in areas like social spending. Although it never really worked out that way (perhaps too many interests relied on a war economy) and few swords were recast as ploughshares, nevertheless, for a short time, there was a certain amount of optimism about the possibilities of the "peace dividend" — the uses to which military spending could be put.

A loose analogy can be made with Ireland. We have had serious economic growth in the last decade and, as noted previously, government ministers have had the luxury of surplus in recent years — making decisions about what to do with windfalls rather than trying to cover shortfalls. Any examination of the Irish psyche must examine the kinds of decisions made about using our "growth dividend" and what the money has been spend on . . . or not, as the case may be. In earlier chapters, I looked at the evidence on changing values and attitudes in Ireland, which of course are tremendously informative. But these may reflect aspirations and even self-delusions in some cases, rather than exclusively telling us who we are now. Or, to put it more succinctly: actions speak louder than words, and financial actions can be deafeningly clear about what our priorities are as a nation. While there may be a debate about whether our government reflects or determines the wishes of society in the laws they enact, either way, in a liberal-democratic system, no attempt to capture change can omit an analysis of the central goals and spending choices of those in power.

It seems reasonable, therefore, to examine the fortunes of a number of different areas which receive central government funding to assess their relative importance at first hand to those holding the purse strings, and at second hand, to the people who vote for them and to whom they answer at election time. In this chapter, I want to look in greatest detail at education. Partly, this is because of some widely held assumptions about the education system in Ireland but also because education is a classical post-materialist priority. It is a long-term "investment" that enriches a citizenry even if it is not regarded as having short-term advantages (although we will see that much of the rhetoric around education presents it as a form of human capital expenditure). The arts will also be examined but in less detail, not because it is less important (since it is the quintessential post-materialist domain) but by its very nature, the "outputs" of the arts are very difficult to assess, leaving the impartial observer only with the inputs or supports to evaluate. I will also briefly review issues around transport, housing and health, because I believe they are illustrative of similar tendencies detectable in the areas of education and the arts.

The Education Investment Revisited

In Chapter 3, the apparent importance of education to Ireland's growth and self-confidence was noted. When a thoughtful economist like Paul Tansey attributes much of Ireland's success to increases over a number of decades in the priority given to education, one would be remiss in ignoring this claim. However, questions were also raised in that section about the literacy of the school population as well as the availability of continued training to people in the workplace. The commitment of successive governments to delivering a share of the growth dividend to education must also be examined in some detail. In this context, it is important to contrast the official rhetoric with some more disinterested assessments of international organisations.

That the Irish education system is excellent is more or less automatically accepted, although the evidence for the claim is harder to find. The Department of Finance's summary of its Stability Programme[1] contained the routine claim that Ireland's economic performance in the 1990s was in part "based on high levels of public investment in physical and human capital" (paragraph 2.6) and that "investment in education and training has raised the quality of the labour force, providing a further impetus to potential growth" (paragraph 2.8). One prop supporting the bitter secondary school teachers' industrial action was the claim that they educated and nurtured the skilled workforce underpinning the economic recovery. As Fintan O'Toole noted (*The Irish Times*, 20 March 2001, E&L supplement, p. 8–9), the ASTI in its PR campaign "claimed that the changes in post-primary education in Ireland in recent years have made . . . the Irish education system the envy of many other countries".

The most confident assertion has been made by the IDA in their webpage[2] dealing with facts about Ireland, where one reads that "Ireland has one of the best education systems in the world". A table is presented comparing investment in education for Ireland with that for eight other countries, showing Ireland in a very positive light. The source of the data is the respected *Education at a Glance: OECD Indicators, 2000*. A closer examination of the table (it appears to be based on OECD Table B1.3, but it is difficult to say since a lot of the figures are misquoted) is useful in deconstructing this claim. The investment level is based on public expenditure on education as a percentage of total *public* expenditure — in other words, the calculation is of education's share of government money, but not the GDP or GNP. A set of figures (Table B1.1a) to be found at an earlier page in

[1] www.irlgov.ie/finance/Budget99/sprog99.htm, Chapter Two (Recent economic performance — Reasons for Ireland's strong growth).

[2] www.idaireland.com/docs/yframes/faivsy.html#education

the OECD publication might have been more informative, but was overlooked by the IDA — this shows that Ireland's direct expenditure on all educational institutions represented only 4.5 per cent of GDP as opposed to an OECD mean of 5.1 per cent, according to 1997 figures (on which the OECD indicators 2000 are based). The comparative figures for 1990 show Ireland at 4.7 per cent against an OECD mean of 4.8 per cent. In other words, our relative position for direct expenditure on education, while slightly below average in 1990, was a good deal better than in 1997 during the boom. Further discouraging news (in Table B1.1d) also failed to make the IDA webpage — this shows that combined public and private expenditure on both primary and secondary education as a percentage of GDP in Ireland was 3.5 per cent, also below the OECD average of 3.9 per cent and below such economic giants as Austria (4.3 per cent), the Czech Republic (3.6 per cent), Finland (3.8 per cent), Mexico (3.9 per cent) and Portugal (4.4 per cent). In the previous OECD indicators document (1997), the data were gathered in 1995. The comparative figure (given on page 65, Table B1.1d again) for Ireland was 3.7 per cent against an OECD mean of 3.7 per cent. Depressingly, this means that in the frothiest years of the economic bubble, we have slid from at least an average position in the OECD to well below average on spending for primary and secondary education.

Of course, it might be argued that education is as valued as ever in Ireland but that changing demography and age profiles can distort the economic figures. The latter is true but not in a way that supports the former. It must be remembered that, in comparison to other OECD countries, Ireland has a disproportionally large younger population, a group for whom education is either compulsory or more likely. The comparative figures provided by OECD Indicators 2000 (table A1.1) show that the 5–14 age group makes up 16 per cent of Ireland's population against an OECD average of 13 per cent, and the respective figures for the 15–19 cohort are 9 per cent for Ireland compared to 7 per cent for the OECD on average. Thus, a quarter of our population was in the 5–19 age group compared to the OECD average of a fifth. We should have been spending substantially more on education in the 1990s than most other comparable countries. In fact, when money invested per student is examined, the IDA claims look even more hollow. The OECD publication (Table B4.1) provides, in US dollars, expenditure per pupil in OECD countries in 1997. In Figure 8.1 below, the figures for education at primary, secondary and tertiary levels for Ireland and the OECD average are presented. As is shown, the spending per pupil at all levels debunks the claims that this society is a world leader in education.

Figure 8.1: Irish and OECD Spending, in Dollars per Pupil, at Three Educational Levels

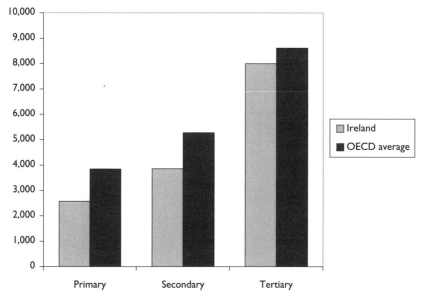

Source: OECD Education at a Glance 2000

A comparison with figures obtained for 1994 and presented in the OECD Indicators for 1997 (from Table B4.1, p. 101 — see Figure 8.2 below) shows that Ireland, if anything, has slipped further behind in spending per pupil. In the midst of the boom and when our economic growth levels were way above the OECD average, Irish spending on secondary and tertiary education levels relative to other OECD countries *actually worsened* (only the abysmal primary spending has improved somewhat but still at just slightly over two-thirds the comparative OECD mean level). An early summary version of the update, OECD *Education at a Glance 2001*, became available in the course of writing this chapter. Again, among OECD countries, Ireland is vastly ahead in terms of GDP growth. However, an assessment of direct expenditure on educational institutions from 1995–1998 shows that growth in educational spending was about two-fifths that of overall economic growth, one of the poorest ratios of any of the OECD countries (Turkey, Greece, Italy, Denmark, and Portugal, for example, are increasing the educational spend at several times the rate of growth).[3]

Figure 8.2: Irish Investment per Pupil as a Percentage of OECD Average (=100%) at Three Education Levels in 1994 and 1997

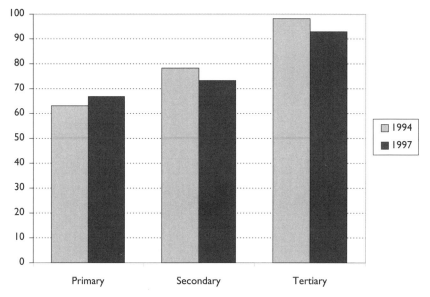

Source: OECD Education at a Glance 2000

And of course, certain consequences must logically follow when investment in education is miserly. Teacher–student ratios are inevitably impacted upon. The OECD statistics also provide some worrying data in this regard (from 1998). The average number of pupils per teacher at the primary level in the OECD is 18.0 while Irish classes have on average 22.6 students per teacher. No other country in the EU has such a poor ratio (not even the much-maligned UK), and only

---

[3] See OECD EAG 2001 Table B2.2 Annex 2.

South Korea and New Zealand manage to cram in more young people per classroom. We also have more primary pupils per class than the *publicly funded* schools of developing countries like Egypt, Jordan, Malaysia, Paraguay, Thailand and Uruguay. Ireland is also well below average for teacher–student ratios at secondary and tertiary levels.

It is difficult to make cross-national comparisons of the educational levels of students from different countries, but clearly Irish students and Irish people generally have poor language skills, especially compared to our often polyglottic continental neighbours. Maths and science provide somewhat less culturally biased sources of comparison. The data indicate that average instruction time per student in these subjects is significantly lower in Ireland than the OECD mean. The OECD indicators provide figures gathered by the IEA/TIMSS (1995) comparing children's performance at maths and science at around the age of ten. Ireland actually does not too badly coming sixth out of 17 countries assessed in maths but tenth in science. Comparing 25 jurisdictions in maths performance at the age of around 14, Ireland is placed fourteenth (table F1.1). A cross-national comparison of literacy in 12 countries by the International Adult Literacy Survey (OECD table A2.3c) of upper secondary/non-university educated groups put Ireland in ninth place.

Given these types of results, why does the notion persist that Ireland has a world-class education system? One might point a finger at the IDA, and their abuse of OECD statistics in a way that is mischievous and misleading to say the least. However, the malaise goes a lot deeper. As a colleague pointed out to me, we in Ireland are the products of this education system and it is unsettling to think of oneself as ill- or under-educated. Most fundamentally, though, there is an unquestioning assumption that the system must be good, because otherwise the unthinkable hoves into view — i.e. the need to invest some additional resources into the system. In fact, the cross-national comparisons of pupil performance may be read positively — although the funding of education in Ireland is at, say, a D-minus level, our students are achieving C-minus level results. Good value for money, but a far cry from a level of excellence. And the deterioration of many indices during the peak of the boom implies that the growth dividend was not "squandered" on education by any means.

The Arts

However difficult it is to measure output in education, particularly between different countries, at least one has certain reasonable benchmarks to think about, such as pupil performance in certain subjects. Furthermore, most individuals in educational institutions are all too accustomed to the tyranny of examination and accept it as normal. Assessing output in the arts is a minefield and distinguishing between good and bad art or even sometimes what is and what is not art are tasks far beyond the ability of this author. However, it is clear that while funding cannot create artistic talent, it can nurture and encourage certain forms of it as well as provide the infrastructure (galleries, cultural centres, museums, etc.) within which it can be displayed, performed or occur. Thus, it is at least reasonable to look at the inputs into the arts from central funding at different times (when government coffers were hollow and later full) to decide if some of the growth dividend was transferred into supporting creativity and expression. Such a move would surely be strong evidence of a post-materialising society moving away from the priorities of "scarcity".

The Arts Council has been the central organisation disbursing in an autonomous way funding received largely from the central government purse. Its publication, *Arts Plan 1999–2001*, notes with approval the increased funding by central government of the annual grant from over £13 million in 1994 to £26 million in 1999. This looks impressive, but some qualifications are in order. First, these figures do not take account of inflation — think of what a typical house sold for in 1994 and then in 1999. Secondly, large portions of this came from National Lottery sources. Thirdly, it tells us nothing about the previous changes in funding. Figure 8.3 below presents the annual percentage change in government funding for the Arts Council on the previous year for the period 1981–1999 (figures collated from the Arts Council Annual Reports 1980–1999).

Figure 8.3: Arts Council Funding from Government, Percentage Increase on Previous Year, 1981–99

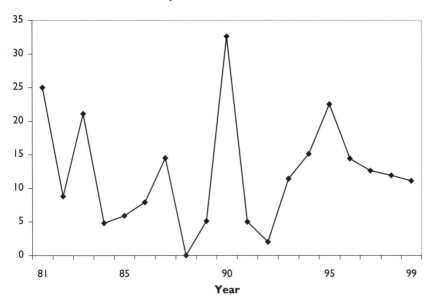

Source: Arts Council Annual Reports 1980-99

The percentages recorded in Figure 8.3 indicate that the late 1990s were certainly not bad years for increased funding although they were not exceptional either. However, given the low levels of inflation at the time and the consistency of improved funding, rather than the more erratic famine and feast of the 1980s, some genuine benefits were surely felt. But again, one must return to the cold reality of cross-national comparisons. The Arts Plan 1999–2001 (p. 7) provides an informative table of public spending on the arts in Ireland per capita and as a percentage of GDP. Data gathered in 1997 showed spending of a measly £12.36 per head in Ireland, placing us second last among nine countries, with only the US bringing up the rear (and the US is well-known for proxy central funding of the arts by tax relief to private donors). The percentage of GDP is presented in Figure 8.4 below.

Figure 8.4: Comparison of Public Spending on Arts as a Percentage of GDP in Nine Jurisdictions

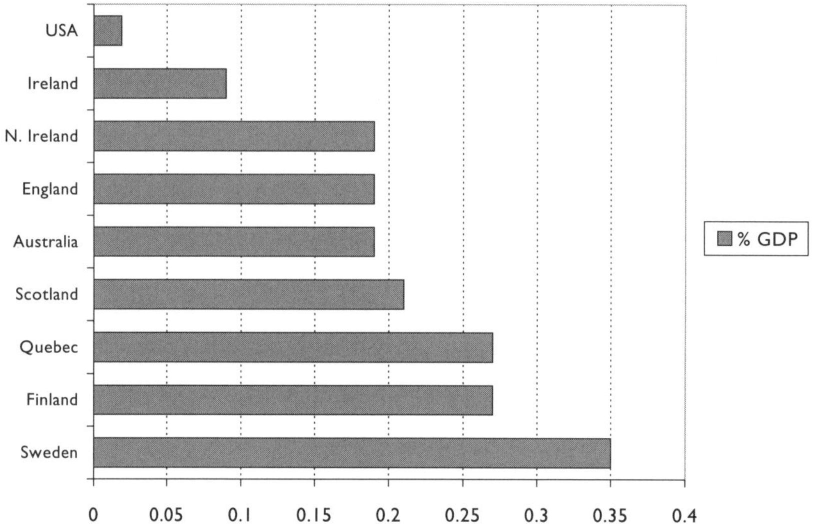

Source: The Arts Plan 1999–2001

The actual percentage for Ireland given in Figure 8.4 above is 0.09 per cent of GDP and that figure is based on 1997 figures. A publication called *Succeeding Better* (1999) prepared by Indecon in association with PriceWaterhouse Coopers cites (on p. 5) an international study estimating that the spending on GDP was actually closer to 0.07 per cent. Whatever the reason for the discrepancy, the message about central funding for the arts in the midst of the economic boom is clear. The spoils of Ireland's extraordinary economic growth would not be used to reverse many years of relatively miserly spending. The artistic community could anticipate increases only as a proportion of the overall cake but need not expect top-up funds to alter its lowly position.

While treading softly on decisions about the merit of aesthetic output in Ireland, one might wonder if the changing culture and economy of Ireland have radically transformed Ireland's international artistic reputation. In truth, there seems to be little evidence that they have. Ardagh (1995) has argued that literature and theatre are the dominant arts in Ireland but with the exception of Northern writers like Heaney and Friel (and perhaps John Banville in the South), there are few who enjoy world renown and critical acclaim. This is disappointing, since it is only since the 1990s that repressive and crude censorship (in direct and indirect forms) has been thoroughly relaxed. The opportunity to "let a hundred flowers bloom" in the post-censorship period was spurned. Indeed, Ireland's areas of "excellence" have been cringeworthy. The country generated boybands at a frightening rate, these grotesques formerly known as artists. Those Irish groups and singers generally accepted as having some integrity and quality emerged in the 1980s, the bad old years. Now, one is not so naïve as to believe that previous generations of Irish musicians were not in it for the money, but wasn't there also a belief in the music? They wanted to get rich, trash hotel rooms *and* make good and interesting music. The current crop, through their management mouthpieces, are very clear about success and its measurement in terms of sales and money. Is it fanciful to imagine that their preference for big bucks over artistic merit mirrors exactly the new Irish value system?

Transport and Housing

Near double-digit growth rates were recorded in Ireland, especially from 1994 onwards (the Department of Finance estimated that the real GNP growth rate increased from 2.7 per cent in 1993 to 7.4 in 1994). If the money didn't go on public expenditure on education or the arts, where was it being spent? Frank McDonald's account of the frenzied infrastructural building in the late 1990s in his book *The Construction of Dublin* provides some clues. Private forms of transport are certainly an important magnet for cash and he estimated that a thousand cars were being added *every week* to an already gridlocked city. The Liffey quays, he observed, are choked very day, the morning rush hour extends to three hours and pollution levels in areas of Dublin and Cork regularly exceed EU maximum levels. McDonald notes that while, in 1996, there were 44,487 newly registered D cars, this climbed to 64,361 in 1999. In 2000,

> . . . such was the double-zero's mesmeric attraction that
> 42,000 new cars were sold throughout the state before the

end of the [first] month, representing a 55 per cent increase
on the figure for the previous January. (p. 28)

Car dealers had never enjoyed such demand for their products. At
the end of 1998, there were 1.5 million vehicles registered in Ireland
compared to just over a million in 1990. While ownership is still
lower than average EU levels, use is much higher. (See more data on
car purchasing in the next chapter.)

Partly the attraction of the car was a symbolic one, promising
freedom and status as well as representing success and conspicuous
consumption. While in the US, a front garden full of cars effectively
(and appallingly) labels the residents as "poor white trash", in the
New Irish Psyche it means, "hey look, we've made it". This ideology
is bolstered by a motor industry, which advertises very heavily to
press the point that a car is no mere humble tool of transport but a
measure of your worth, your sexiness and even your individual identity. Car culture advocates a message, suggests Sadhbh O'Neill, that
"my journey is more important than yours" (quoted in McDonald,
2000: 31). And if that is true for any car, then one's journey takes
special priority in a swish car. Allen (2000) cites figures on sales of
new luxury cars in Ireland — they increased from 2,089 in 1993 to
5,789 only four years later in 1997, i.e. almost trebling.

However, the image of the car and its mystification by the advertising industry are only part of the problem. The downgrading of the
public transport system, with its message that "buses are for losers"
(the Dort is just about alroight) is the other side of the coin. As
McDonald points out, the rule of thumb for successive governments
was "that public transport loses money, therefore we shouldn't invest in public transport" (p. 30). This has led to doubling of passen-
gers on many rail lines, decrepit trains and the lowest level of public
subsidy for Dublin Bus of any transport system in a Europe capital (at
4 per cent of running costs). Carrot-and-stick strategies to force
people out of their cars only work when the carrot, a reasonable
alternative form of transport, actually exists. But in Ireland, the
steady, patient work required to build these falls victim to spectacular high-profile plans for "Bertie Bowls" and other flagship projects.
In the absence of decent and interconnected public transport sys-

tems, people have taken to private transport and are willing to accept the ulcer-inducing jams, personal expense and environmental damage in return for some privacy. (As an exercise, count the number of cars containing more than one adult in a typical rush hour in Ireland — my unscientific sampling puts it at about 10 per cent.)

The traffic problem is inseparable from and exacerbated by the housing crisis. Providing a list of recent high prices achieved by house sales in the bijou areas of Dublin, Cork or Limerick is inherently misleading (the figures will look dated in six months) as well as unnecessary (the topic has been done to death in the same anxious conversations endured by so many). But it is clear that many of the paper increases in salaries and wages have disappeared in chasing spiralling mortgage and rent costs. Allen (2000: 94) cites the finding of the Drudy commission on housing that the ratio of house prices in Dublin to the average industrial wage in 1994, at the beginning of the boom, was just over 4:1. Four years later, the equivalent ratio was 8:1. The public provision of housing, however, only amounted to 7 per cent in that year. Apart from the financial difficulties caused by spiralling prices, McDonald points out that geographical distortions were also inevitable. The Greater Dublin Area continues to become more and more bloated, impacting on the development and life of towns as distant as Gorey, Mullingar and Tullamore, as they become drawn into a huge region from which it is now considered perfectly reasonable to commute to Dublin. The demand for large chunks of individual and inviolable living space means that most of Kildare, Louth and Wicklow are already threatened with soulless suburbanisation. See the next chapter for further discussion of changes in housing.

Health

The final area I want to examine is that of public expenditure on health. Displeasure, even despair, at the inability of the health system in Ireland to deliver adequate care in a *reasonable* timeframe and at affordable cost has been widely expressed. It is one of those areas which even those who have been most vocal in their praise of the growth of the economy have acknowledged as poor, to put it mildly. The neglect of the health system, as we shall see, is perfectly in line with much thinking on public spending but the statistics make surprising reading, surpassing even the failure to re-invest in the education and arts systems. The context of health funding in Ireland is best described in a comparative way and Eurostat, the European Commission's data collection arm, usefully published its comprehensive *Key Data on Health, 2000*, which provides the basis of an overview. Firstly, Ireland's demographic profile should be noted. The age dependency ratio of the country (the population aged 0–14 and 65 plus as a percentage of the total population) is much higher than the EU average — this means that relatively speaking, the country requires higher levels of funding, since people categorised as age-dependent are more likely to seek medical attention. However, the number of physicians per 100,000 population is way below the EU average (Eurostat Table 6.1.4); and in fact, in the last year for which comparative data are available, of the 15 EU countries, only the UK had a less favourable ratio. In 1997, Ireland's ratio of 213 physicians per 100,000 population can be contrasted to Portugal's 306 or Greece's 410. The latest UN Human Development Report showed that Ireland in 1999 continued to lie in fourteenth place out of 15 EU countries in this regard (2001: 158) with Italy having an astonishing two and a half times greater number of physicians per 100,000 population (Ireland had 219, Italy had 554).

Economic growth should have enabled the country to improve funding for the medical services but, as we can see, this opportunity has so far been spurned (although some recent signs point to a possible change — see Chapter 12). Figure 8.5 compares the total expenditure (i.e. private and public) as a percentage of GDP in Ireland from 1993–1997 to the EU average.

While in 1980, Ireland spent a higher percentage of its GDP on health care than the EU-15, the relative decline of the medical spend in the 1990s can be seen in Figure 8.5. It might be protested that Ireland's GDP was increasing in this period, therefore making it more difficult for medical spending to maintain its share. But this is precisely the issue. It should have been axiomatic that health at least stay at its current proportion of spending (and in fact should have been increased), so that Ireland's population as a whole could have directly experienced the growth dividend as a health dividend. This was not to be. In terms of spending on health per capita in 1993, at the beginning of the largest economic boom in the state's history, Ireland lay in twelfth place of the EU 15. Four years later, at the end of 1997, and Ireland's position on the same index was . . . twelfth. (Eurostat Table 6.4.5)

Figure 8.5: EU Average and Irish Expenditure in Health as a Percentage of GDP, 1993–97

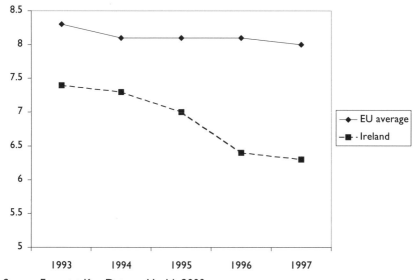

Source: Eurostat Key Data on Health 2000

These statistical returns are not mere abstractions. The impact of funding decisions is direct and practical, including chronic staff shortages and industrial action by nurses. In terms of average length of stay in hospital, there was a continuing progressive slide from 10 days in 1980 to 7 days in 1996 (the latest date for which comparable data are available in Eurostat). The EU average in 1996 was much higher, at a mean length of 12 days. Number of hospital beds in Ireland — a far from abstract statistic — declined from 31,106 in 1980 to 18,114 in 1999. It meant that, while in 1993, there were 56 beds per 10,000 population, by 1999, there were only 48 (Table 6.2.7). And not surprisingly, in a European-wide survey of satisfaction with national health services in 1998, only a smaller percentage of Greeks,

Italians and Portuguese reported themselves as "very satisfied" with their health service than the 5.1 per cent of Irish respondents. The EU average satisfaction rate was almost double that (Eurostat Table 6.2.19).

The Missing Millions — Putting the Picture Together

How should these trends in Irish society be understood? Allen (2000) has argued that a book written in 1992 by John Kenneth Galbraith has seduced, or at least had a tremendous impact, on the thinking of many Irish intellectuals. Galbraith's book was called *The Culture of Contentment* and Allen contends that the contrast depicted in the book of a US society split between a contented majority, demanding tax reductions, and an impoverished minority requiring additional government funding, was adopted wholesale by Irish thinkers. Allen argues that the importation of this intellectual model was unjustified — that only a small minority of the Irish population has benefited in any real way from the boom. For Allen, the truth is less palatable — we don't have a selfish majority leaving behind a small and miserable underclass — rather we have what he calls a discontented majority. This includes most blue- and white-collar workers as well as the very poorest who have much more in common with each other as they struggle to survive while a small elite obtain a greater share of the resources.

This is an important argument but it is undermined by a (deliberate?) misreading of Galbraith's position — although it may be an accurate reflection of some who seek to use his analysis for their own purposes. Galbraith makes it explicitly clear in a number of different places in his book that he is not referring to a majority of US citizens when he speaks of a contented majority — rather, he stresses that

> . . . they are now a majority, not of all citizens but of those who actually vote. A convenient reference is needed for those so situated. . . . They will be called the Contented Majority, the Contented Electoral Majority, or more spaciously, the Culture of Contentment. There will be adequate reiteration that this does not mean they are a majority of all those eligible to vote. (Galbraith, 1992: 15)

Given Galbraith's appreciation that probably a majority of adults residing in the US don't vote (when one considers non-voting, non-registration and illegal immigrants), it is abundantly clear that he is speaking of a contented small minority, more or less explicitly "the top 20 per cent [living] in conditions of some comfort [and accruing] 51.8 per cent of all income before taxes" (p. 14). He also makes it clear that this "majority" are living in short-term contentment only, frequently threatened by the long-term possibility of recession, and the violence of the disgruntled poor. In fact, his 20 per cent of people who are doing very well looks very similar to the "15 or 20 percent of the Irish population" that Allen (p. 68) speaks of as the new Irish middle class.

In reality, Galbraith's description of the US offers uncanny similarities to the Irish scenario. Most important of these is remorseless hostility to progressive taxation and public spending. It may be an act of long-term stupidity not to plough the proceeds of the boom back into education, health, public transport, housing, infrastructure and the arts, but in the short term, who cares? The hatred of taxation has become visceral. At least partially, the corruption and cronyism of the political class are to blame — people will only support taxation if they feel it is being collected and used fairly. Clearly in Ireland that hasn't happened — taxation has often been just for the little people, the schmucks. The consequence has been an embracing of policies and political currents advocating the most crass tax-cutting. While Allen may argue that the turn to Thatcherism is being done *onto* the people, in a stealthy way, with the support of the trade union misleaders, Galbraith's notion of a participating and co-opted majority of those who are politically active is more accurate. The truth is that the majority of voters (and that's much closer to an actual majority of Irish citizens than in the US case) supported in parliamentary and/or union elections the rush-and-grab strategy. We preferred the term "social partnership" over Reaganism or Thatcherism, but that didn't change its nature. People are not unaware of the shortcomings in the publicly financed domains in Ireland, especially not in health. There was no conspiracy from the top but rather a Faustian pact.

The writer and economist Paul Sweeney (in an article in *The Irish Times* in April 2001) has argued, accurately, that public spending in Ireland has diminished rapidly and is heading to the level of Manila, rather than Boston, let alone Berlin. However, he also claims that "most citizens will happily pay a few pence more in tax to get good public transport, and access to health care and decent schooling for their children". Really? It seems more likely that the Irish people have accepted that education, health, public transport and so on will continue to be funded only at bare subsistence levels. The good news is that more can thus afford a shiny new car — the bad news is they'll have to use it with all the other private travellers every day commuting 60 miles to Dublin. The New Irish Psyche is a right-wing and short-term mindset.

Allen cites the analysis by O'Hearn (1998) to suggest that, counter to ideology, spending on private consumption by individuals has declined in relative terms in Ireland during the boom. He adds that "if there has been a fall in the share of the national economy going into general consumption, the luxury consumption of the rich and the new middle class has increased quite dramatically" (p. 68). He may be correct on the latter point — as noted in Chapter 3, the current Minister for Finance holds, unusually for Ireland, a real commitment to a neo-liberal ideology and has ensured that the better-off continue to maintain and indeed increase their share of the growth. However, it is not true to claim that general private consumption levels have not risen dramatically. Unlike the areas mentioned above, like health and education, they have kept pace (after an initial sluggishness) with comparative GDP and GNP levels. The final diagram in this chapter (Figure 8.6 — based on the CSO National Income and Expenditure Figures, 2000, Table 6.1) makes this clear. Where did the growth dividend go? We, the consumers, especially the wealthy ones, spent it. In Chapter 9, consumer spending is examined in greater detail.

Figure 8.6: Growth in GNP and Personal Consumption Spending, 1993–99

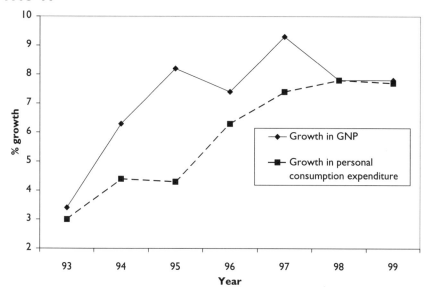

Source: CSO National Income and Expenditure Figures 2000

Chapter 9

CHIPS WITH EVERYTHING: THE CONSUMPTION EXPLOSION

In the previous chapter, it was argued that the last decade generated a rapid increase in private accumulation and consumption of goods. This point was made in opposition to Allen's (2000) claim that individual consumption had not grown substantially. The purpose of this chapter is to describe Irish spending patterns in some detail. It provides, as we shall see, some strong evidence for Galbraith's "consumption" thesis, that growth has led to sharp excess. In so far as possible, this claim will be demonstrated by available data. As noted before, the problem with the human memory is that it reconstructs *a* past rather than recalling *the* past. As regards testing hypotheses, this can work in opposing ways. For example, for many, the "Thatcherite and Reaganite eras" evoke an image of excess and greed in the UK and US. But was this actually the case or is that a now-agreed stereotype of the time? (Actually, it was the case, as it happens.) Similarly, it is easy to notice new restaurants and bars opening up, but cognitive psychologists have demonstrated that humans are notoriously poor at interpreting non-events or non-happenings — retail outlets now closed or disappeared that once were popular, for example. So, in thinking about change in Ireland in areas like shopping, buying, eating and drinking, we need to leave our impressions to one side and where possible, use reliable figures. Simply "sensing" that everywhere is busier than it used to be is an interesting but not necessarily reliable observation.

Let us begin in unapologetic metropolitan-chauvinist mode and review some Dublin-based information. Phonebooks are a fairly exhaustive database delivered free to our door. The Golden Pages obviously provides an index of commercial interests, grouped by type of service. Since businesses must pay to be in it, it is not necessarily a perfect census of all possible commercial interests. Nonetheless, it should provide at least a rough measure of what's around. The simple but unglamorous research task of examining the 01 area (mainly Dublin) Golden Pages for 1995/96 and 2000/01 was undertaken. Specifically, the number of entries for booksellers, public houses, licensed restaurants, fast food (unlicensed) restaurants and off licences were counted. The increase for the five sectors between 1995 and 2000 is discernible in Figure 9.1. (In order to make comparison of relative change easier, the 1995 starting point for each has been standardised to 100.)

Figure 9.1: Proportional Increase in Entries for Five Sectors in the 01 Area, 1995–2000 (1995 level standardised to 100)

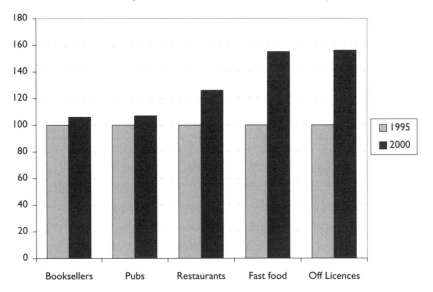

Source: Golden Pages

As Figure 9.1 demonstrates, growth occurred across many different sectors. It was weakest in bookseller units and public houses. However, one should be cautious about the latter — pub licences in Dublin are notoriously expensive and/or difficult to acquire. Increased consumer demand for pubs is often met by turning a small bar into a superpub rather than opening a new one. A very sharp demand, though, in the space of five years has created many more businesses providing food and alcohol for quick and easy purchase — fast food joints and off-licences.

Of course, the number of various businesses in the Golden Pages for the Dublin area hardly provides irrefutable evidence of change in and of itself. Some businesses may be less busy, others decide not to advertise, etc. and of course, despite what people in the Dublin area may believe, life, as we know it, does not end at that county border. More detailed national statistics are available from the EU's statistical service, Eurostat. The most recent available at the time of writing for many sorts of information only run to 1997 or 1998, but they still tend to show an explosion in basic consumption in Ireland. Change in volume of consumption of various goods is the statistic used in the next group of charts. An alternative measure, proportion of national income, will be relied upon later in the chapter. Both are valuable but different measures (where the national income has grown rapidly, then even stability in proportional consumption of a good means that in real terms, its consumption is increasing).

Quantity and quality of diet invariably reflect the purchasing power of the public. An examination of the changing consumption levels of meat in eight EU countries for which data are available up to 1997 (with the 1990 level standardised at 100) showed that it increased by 12 per cent in Ireland in that period while it declined in Belgium, France, Greece, Austria and Italy, stayed constant in Finland and increased in Holland by 6 per cent. Again, one must be cautious in interpreting the statistics — eating meat is not just a function of money but also of taste, health beliefs and sometimes, personal morality. But the basic additional intake of all foodstuffs is clear from the whole range of Eurostat statistics, where Ireland is ranked the highest or second highest in increased food consumption across all the basic categories (although the Irish population, like most other EU ones, has reduced consumption of sugars and fats). Consumption of milk, cheese and eggs was up 11 per cent, potatoes and tubers 19 per cent and fruit and vegetables 33 per cent (See Figure 9.2 below).

Figure 9.2: Consumption of Foodstuffs in Ireland, 1990-97 (1990=100)

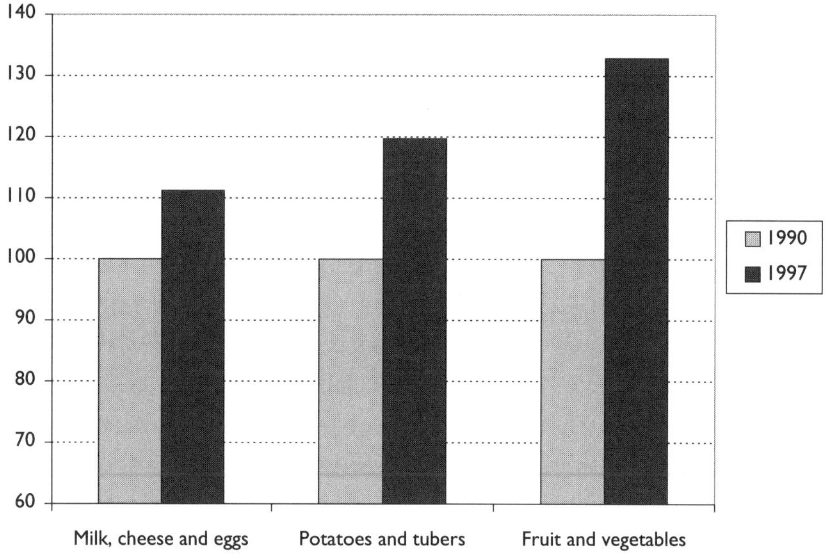

Source: Eurostat Yearbook 2000

So a lot of the new purchasing power went into fairly basic things. Much of the economic growth in individual consumption was spent literally on things to consume. We will return to this issue later, but another widely cited aspect of change in modern Ireland has been in the area of housing/accommodation. The housing boom, or crisis, depending on whether you're a seller or buyer, is the aspect of economic change that has probably captured peoples' imaginations more than any other. The excitement of hearing that your once modest two-up two-down is now valued at some sizeable fraction of a million pounds is tempered only by having to listen to your grasping offspring whine about the prices. A lot of the housing hype is a function only of market forces and not much more interesting than that. However, one must also recognise that, at least partially, it reflects quite a fundamental shift in living modes, values and standards. As demand for privacy and space has grown, inevitably there is pressure on current property prices alongside a resigned acceptance to long-term apartment living. Figure 9.3a diagrammatically presents the declining average number of occupants per house in Ireland in the last two decades.

Figure 9.3a: Declining Average Number of Occupants per Household in Ireland

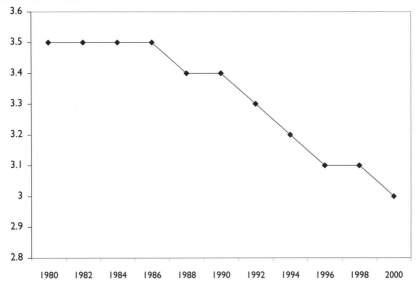

Source: Euromonitor

Naturally, this change is not just about taste in houses or space but also reflects a transition of family size and structure in Ireland in that period (see Chapter 6). If a general "convergence" thesis is true and Irish society can be expected to slowly grow more similar to other European societies, then this decline in occupancy number will continue. As Figure 9.3b shows, the general European average is a good deal lower.

Figure 9.3b: Average Number of Occupants per Household in EU Countries (2000)

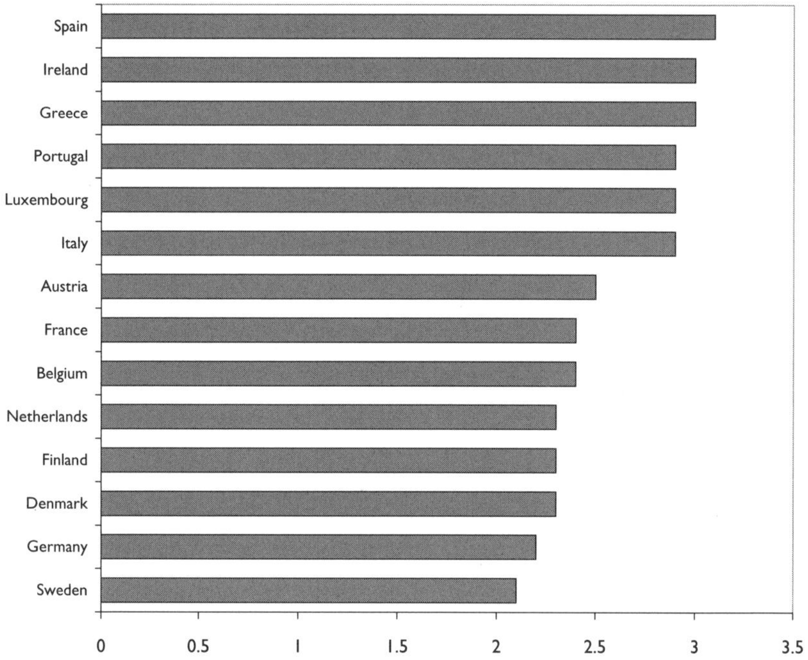

Source: Euromonitor

The evidence so far supports an argument (one that I will return to at the end of this chapter) that greater income does not necessarily produce more post-materialist orientations but rather more sophisticated forms of materialism. For example, shelter or accommodation is at once a basic need but potentially also a very sophisticated product. And rather than growing less interested in a basic need like housing when one grows wealthier, one may instead choose to invest in it both financially and culturally.

Let Them Eat Chicken Tikka Masala!

It can be argued that a person could live on a basic, nutritious but unexciting diet or might pursue eating patterns that were more exotic or sophisticated. The trends in Ireland are operating in the latter direction over the last decade. Changes in the number of Golden Pages entries in the greater Dublin area over a five-year period were presented at the beginning of the chapter. By that admittedly crude measure, growth in literal consumption was dramatic. More convincing national data are available from marketing experts whose livelihood depends on them making reliable predictions about trends in consumption and spending patterns. The Mintel Report on Ireland's "eating out" market (1999) certainly confirms that in the past decade, "food for the household has decreased as a proportion of consumer spending" (p. 2). On the other hand, consumer spending on meals outside the home "grew by 47 per cent between 1995 and 1999". This includes restaurant meals, other sit-down meals in formal outlets, pub food and fast food. The final group, fast food and takeaways, have expanded most quickly.

It is instructive to compare the growth of eating out across a number of European countries in the 1990s. The Eurostat Yearbook 2000 provides data up to 1997 for eight EU countries. Figure 9.4 below presents the change between 1990 and 1997 in expenditure on restaurants, cafés and hotels (with 1990 = 100).

Figure 9.4: Change in Expenditure on Restaurants, Cafés and Hotels (volume indices, 1990=100)

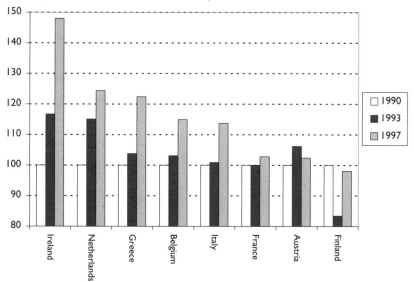

Source: Eurostat Yearbook 2000

Unfortunately, no national data are to hand to endorse the claim that the restaurant/fast food market has grown qualitatively as well as quantitatively and that diverse and ethnic cuisines are now mainstream in a way that was not the case a decade ago. It's also difficult to provide evidence that even relatively conservative eating venues such as hotel restaurants are providing a much more diverse set of eating options. But both are certainly true. Robin Cook, the former British Secretary of Foreign Affairs, made a well-intentioned, but perhaps patronising, claim that the national dish of Britain was now Chicken Tikka Masala (by which he intended to show that integration of minority and majority cultures was progressing well). In Ireland, in the past, one might have made the same claim about Chinese food as a national-ethnic cuisine. But the palate for exotic foodstuff here has gone well beyond Italian restaurants or Chinese takeaways. In June 2001, on a webpage styling itself "the definitive guide to eating out in Ireland", was a section on newly opened restaurants, i.e. within the previous few months — of the 15 listed, five were Thai or Asian Fusion. Was there a single Thai restaurant in Ireland in 1990?

Here be Flagons

Not surprisingly, alcohol consumption also increased in quantity as well as becoming more diverse. In Figure 9.5, the change in consumption of alcohol across the same eight EU countries as before (plus Germany) is presented — have a guess before looking at it where the increase is most pronounced.

Figure 9.5: Consumption of Alcohol by Volume (1990 = 100)

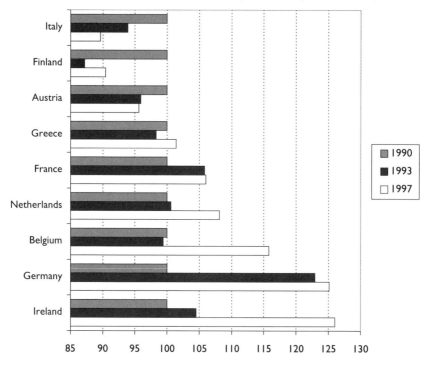

Source: Eurostat Yearbook 2000

Ireland has grown most rapidly (although it only sneaks top place in Figure 9.5 from Germany). The overall alcohol consumption rate in Ireland for population size had previously been close to the European average. This disguised quite high rates of individual drinking through the presence of a large number of teetotallers as well as a low ratio of wine to beer consumption (wine typically has treble the alcohol volume of beer). The pattern of the last decade has now changed this, with wine consumption almost doubling between 1994 and 1999 (Mintel Report on Alcoholic Drinks — Ireland 1999, Figure 5) while beer consumption grew steadily and spirits only slightly.

You are what you eat (and drink) is the popular if dubious slogan. It is interesting to examine the correlation of economic and physical growth in the Irish people — all that extra fast food, Thai chicken and alcohol-enriched wine has to go somewhere, after all. In 1999, the Irish Universities Nutrition Alliance carried out an All Ireland

Food Consumption Survey. In its report of the survey findings, the Alliance also included data from 1990 gathered via the Irish National Nutrition Survey. This makes it possible to examine changes in anthropometry (human size) and from this the BMI (Body Mass Index)[1] distribution of the population. Using WHO categorisations, the BMI scores in turn can be used to estimate the proportions of overweight and obese people in the population.[2] Figure 9.6 below compares the changes for different groups according to sex and age between 1990 and 1999.

Figure 9.6: Percentage of Overweight and Obese Adults in Ireland, 1990 and 1999

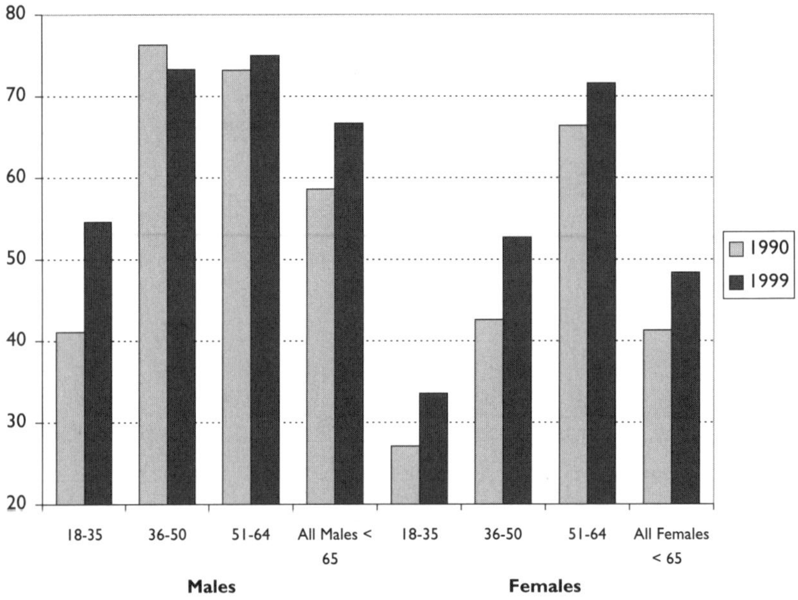

Source: All Ireland Food Consumption Survey

The differences in Figure 9.6 are substantial across the decade. While not overly healthy to begin with, especially older groups and males, the consumption boom of the 1990s has produced a situation where over half the adult Irish population is overweight. Figures for

[1] Calculated as body weight in kilograms divided by body height in metres squared.

[2] "Overweight" is defined as a BMI > 25 and ≤ 30. "Obese" is defined as a BMI > 30.

obesity only (not presented in this diagram) show a trebling in the proportion of younger males and middle-aged females categorised as such when beginning and end of the decade are compared. In passing, it might be suggested that the greatest threat to mainstream Irish health is not the gaunt skeletal fashion models, supposedly influencing us to take up starvation diets. Rather, it is an expanding financial capacity for a rich diet accompanied by an ever-more sedentary lifestyle.

But of course, extra purchasing power was not solely directed towards eating. The increase in consumption of clothing and shoes almost doubled (an increase of 83.2 per cent measured in volume of goods rather than value or percentage of consumption) between 1990 and 1997 (Eurostat Yearbook 2000: 173). This increase, at its most rapid between the years 1995 and 1997, towers above any of the other EU countries — the closest is the UK with 35.4 per cent while the EU average was 7 per cent. Virtually all the indices measuring rates of increase of consumption point in this explosive upward direction for Ireland in the 1990s while the EU average remains modest. So, for example, consumption of "furniture, furnishings and household equipment" increased in that period in Ireland by 47.2 per cent against an EU average of 12.3 per cent (Eurostat Yearbook 2000: 174). The Euromonitor data service provides very detailed information on trends in spending across most international countries. Examining consumer expenditure in constant IR£ for an arbitrarily selected set of goods, the greatest increase between 1993 and 1999 recorded was in "hairdressing and beauty care" (171 per cent increase), followed by housing (151 per cent), financial services (112 per cent), petrol and oil (83 per cent), household cleaning products (48 per cent), "books, newspapers and magazines" (16 per cent) and "jewellery, silverware, watches and clocks, travel goods" (minus 4 per cent). The retail price index increase for all items in the same period in Ireland was 50.3 per cent (Euromonitor 2001).

Advertising expenditure per EU country for the years 1994 to 1999 is also provided in the Euromonitor database. Not unexpectedly, its growth in Ireland in that time has been very rapid and the increase is second only in the EU to that of Portugal for the period, followed by Italy and the UK, with France and Germany bringing up the rear.

R u txt msgng?

One would be wrong, however, to assume that purchasing has lacked any technological sophistication or that it is merely limited to items for immediate consumption. The world-wide communications revolution has not left Ireland unscathed. Internet usage, for example, has exploded from an estimated 2,000 tentative users in 1991 to 665,000 in 2000 (Euromonitor, 2001). Mobile phones have moved from the realms of elitist hi-tech to mainstream to will-you-switch-that-bloody-thing-off in the briefest number of years. The growth rate has been phenomenal in Ireland — from 25,000 units in 1990 to 1,408,000 in 1999 (Euromonitor). Technology once limited to government ministers and captains of industry is now in the nimble hands of adolescents. (Apparently, student walkouts occurring in Ireland in early 2001 during the secondary teachers' strikes were largely co-ordinated via mobile phone text messages.) It is clear that Ireland has not been unusual in this regard. In a European context, typically countries had mobile phone ownership rates of about half the adult population, and climbing, at the close of the twentieth century.

Where Ireland did grow well above average was in the slightly more old-fashioned part of the communications/infrastructural area — car ownership. The use of higher incomes to fund access to a new car was one of the most characteristic features of Irish consumption (see also previous chapter). The rates of change between 1994 and 1999 for EU countries are presented in Figure 9.7.

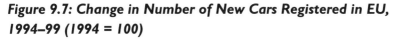

Figure 9.7: Change in Number of New Cars Registered in EU, 1994–99 (1994 = 100)

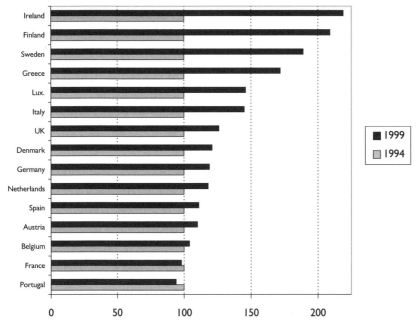

Source: Euromonitor

In defence, the numbers in Figure 9.7 must be taken in context. Irish ownership of cars has historically been low compared to an EU average and the race for ownership is in many ways a race to catch up. However, Irish usage, as opposed to ownership, of cars was already well above other EU countries (where many people have cars but do not use them on a daily basis) — hence the relatively high levels of congestion and traffic accidents.

Overall, there is a lot of consumption at the high-tech end of the market, as represented by Internet usage, mobile phone access and new car ownership. Might this be taken as some evidence for the existence of "post-modern" or "post-materialist" consumption? At the risk of falling prey to old-fogeyism, one suspects that much of the content of mobile phone communications fails to go beyond the typical "I'm on the train", or more aptly in Ireland, "I'm in my new car". The qualitative leap, to make mobile phones a powerful interactive computing tool, has yet to occur and even when it does, they may not often be used to their full potential. Of course, it can be argued that increased dialogue and conversation on the phone must enrich society, but . . . is it unfair to think that many people with mobile phones might be more enriched by switching off their phones occasionally and enjoying a rare few moments of contemplation instead? Increased usage of the web also promises much but undoubtedly it will take most of us time to learn to appreciate its potential rather than to use it in an aimless, puerile or smutty way.

That's Entertainment

In an interesting report on Irish spending habits, a Mintel report (2000) suggests that the statistics contradict "the mistaken assumption that the 'cultural' aspects of consumer spending are increasing in importance" in Ireland (Out-of-home Entertainment report, p. 1). "Culture" in this regard is intended to mean general out-of-home entertainment and not necessarily what we sometimes call "high culture". The report continues,

> . . . a number of consumer spending areas have grown rapidly during the Republic's economic boom, notably house-buying, DIY, clothing and holidays abroad, but the average household only devoted 0.7 per cent of its expenditure to entertainment outside the home in 1999, down from 0.85 per cent in 1995. (pp. 1–2)

(Naturally, one should be mindful of reasons for that statistical decline — given the overall increase in consumer spending, it is unlikely that spending on outside entertainment declined in real terms but merely stayed constant while spending on other areas grew.) In-home entertainment, such as broadcast television and video rental, was a key competitor, while eating out and sport provided the external rivals. The report claims that theatre, concert halls, "dancing", bingo, school and church functions were in relative decline while only the cinema kept pace with growth in other domains. Cinema admissions in the 1991–1999 period jumped from about 8 million to about 12.5 million. About three-quarters of cinema-goers are in the 15–34 age range group. The top-grossing films tended to be the "Hollywood Blockbuster", according to the Mintel report. And indeed a list of the top ten films based on value-takings in Ireland in the 1990s includes, for example, no cinematic studies of nineteenth-century bourgeois families in the provinces in slow decline, a theme adored by French film-makers. Instead we find *Titanic, Jurassic Park, Independence Day, Star Wars: The Phantom Menace,* and *Austin Powers: The Spy Who Shagged Me.* While cinema screens have grown more numerous and bigger (or should that be "mega"), the variety of films has declined.

Synthesis

A more important task than counting the audience for *Austin Powers,* or the number of tequila slammers sold in 1994, or any other individual statistic, is forming a coherent model of consumption patterns in Ireland and thus trying to obtain a sense of where overall trends are leading. The Euromonitor service, for example, provides an overall picture of consumption growth for the years 1992–1997 for various areas of consumption. The results are displayed in Figure 9.8.

Figure 9.8: Percentage Growth in Consumer Spending by Sector, 1992–1997

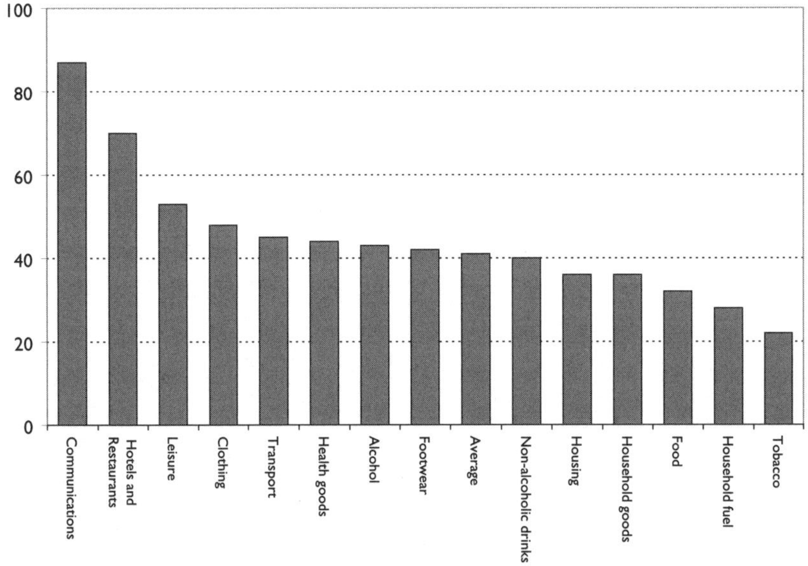

Source: Euromonitor "Consumer Lifestyles" Report, p. 37

The context of Figure 9.8 is crucial — all the major sectors of consumer spending are up. Attempts to deny the huge individual consumerist aspects of the boom are a nonsense. The only questions to be answered are relativist ones — where were the increases most and least rapid. The diagram above provides support for the claim in the Euromonitor report that

> . . . although spending has increased in every sector, viewed as a proportion of total expenditure, spending was down in a handful of categories. . . . Consumers prefer to spend their additional disposable income on non-essential items rather than spending more on everyday goods. (Consumer Lifestyles Ireland: 37)

In October 1917, the Bolsheviks took power in Russia following a revolution in Petrograd and Moscow. Not widely known was the defencelessness of the revolution in the first weeks, caused by a massive binge among the residents of these cities. In Petrograd, the Bolsheviks were forced to destroy huge numbers of bottles of fine wines, collected by the Romanovs over the generations of their reign. This was simply to prevent their own supporters, the city's workers, sailors and soldiers, from getting their hands on the stuff, and thus hopefully sobering them up.[3] Elsewhere, towards the end of another World War, the writer Evelyn Waugh, in the preface to his celebrated book, *Brideshead Revisited* (1993 edition), comments that he thought about removing the perceived excessive and gratuitous references to food and drink in the text.

> It was a bleak period of present privations and threatening disaster — the period of soya beans and Basic English — and

---

[3] In the appendices to John Reed's famous book, *Ten Days that Shook the World*, one finds the following — "The Council of People's Commissars appointed a Commissar for the Fight Against Drunkenness, who, besides mercilessly putting down the wine riots, destroyed hundreds of thousands of bottles of liquor. The Winter Palace cellars, containing rare vintages valued at more than five million dollars, were at first flooded, and then the liquor was removed to Cronstadt and destroyed" (Appendix 7 to Chapter 11). See also I. Deutscher's biography of Trotsky, 1954, vol. I, p. 322, "The grotesque sequel to the October insurrection, a sequel to which historians rarely give attention, was a prodigious, truly elemental orgy of mass drunkenness with which the freed underdog celebrated his victory."

> in consequence the book is infused with a kind of gluttony, for
> food and wine, . . . and for rhetorical and ornamental lan-
> guage, which now with a full stomach I find distasteful.

In both of these cases, the tumult, shortages and hungers of wartime
produced a feverish desire for, and uncontrollable intake of, provi-
sions when available. Although Ireland did not experience a war in
the 1980s, nor chronic gluttony in the 1990s, it is not unfair to say
that a milder version of this action/reaction occurred. The 1980s
were a bleak decade of belt-tightening (for most of us anyway) and
it's not surprising, blameworthy or unacceptable that one of the first
responses to having some disposable income was to direct it towards goods for immediate gratification.

What are unacceptable and insidious are self-illusions. The primary goal of Irish society in the 1990s was consumerism, and ac-
quisitive materialism, and this must be honestly and frankly
acknowledged. When the opportunity came around, the first thing
we wanted to do with additional income was to play catch-up with
Europe in terms of private, individual, consumption — health, education, and indeed virtually any of the sectors supported by the public
purse and ultimately taxation, would have to wait. The dash for
goods and services could not. Prior to that, we were not an obviously materialistic society. It turns out, though, that it wasn't for the
want of trying — the sluggishness of the economy and the perpetual
productive downturn prior to the late 1980s made reluctant ascetics
of us all. We weren't indifferent to the seductions of wealth; we just
didn't have any money.

In terms of a theoretical understanding of the consequences of
rapid financial growth, Ireland certainly provides evidence for the
Galbraith thesis that a constant pursuance of individual consumption
is often preferred over publicly funded projects. The characteristic of
that consumption is the favouring of quantity over quality, first and
foremost. In Ireland, the only sign of qualitative development was the
demand for more sophisticated housing, eating and drinking. Culturally, fairly passive, old-fashioned and unchallenging forms of entertainment like television, video and mainstream cinema have
benefited, without a corresponding growth in "high culture". It may

be, though, that too much is expected too soon of Ireland's development and that the timing, background and perceived longevity of economic and political stability all play a role. This notion of the *context* in which growth occurs will be considered in Chapter 12.

Chapter Ten

LA DIFFÉRENCE VIVE! GENDER AND CHANGE

Show me the Money

So far, we have concerned ourselves mainly with an analysis of Irish society as a whole. But social change often has an uneven nature and what may be of tremendous significance — for example, among one age group or social class — can leave another barely disturbed. A potentially vital discriminating dimension in this regard is gender. To what extent have men and women been transformed by socio-economic change? Or to put the question another way, given that women have historically been less directly integrated into the formal economy, has economic growth exercised as much influence on their lives and attitudes as it has on men? Information supplied by the Central Statistics Office tells a story of rapid transformation. In Figure 10.1a below, the changes in numbers employed of males and females in the last quarter of each year from 1997 to 2000 are displayed.

A number of things should be noted about the data in Figure 10.1a. First, there is some evidence of convergence. In 1997, female workers made up 67 per cent of the corresponding male figure. In 2000, that percentage is 70 per cent. A modest change certainly, but then three years is not a long time. Longer term, in 1976 the number of working females was 212,000 and in 1996, it was 488,000. The transition has been gradual, Fabian even, not revolutionary but impressive nonetheless. Paid employment is psychologically empowering and must create the potential for greater gender equality (and less female deference to men), in day-to-day interaction.

Figure 10.1a: Numbers (in thousands) of Males and Females in the Irish Workforce

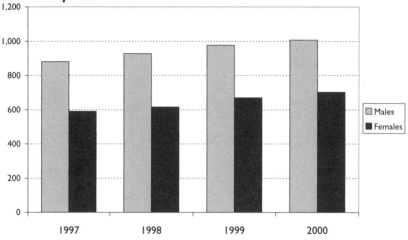

Source: CSO

However, female employment differs from male employment not just quantitatively but qualitatively. Much of it, for example, is part-time. In Figure 10.1b below, the employment numbers have been broken down by gender as well as by type.

Figure 10.1b: Numbers (in thousands) of Full-time and Part-time Males and Females in the Irish Workforce

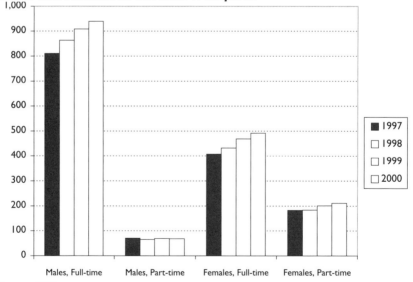

Source: CSO

In fact, one reasonable interpretation of the data in Figure 10.1b is that the boom drew more males than females into work — the numbers of full-time males in employment have increased in raw terms more than those of females. About 30 per cent of female employment is part-time, compared to just over 5 per cent of male. And the female labour force is much smaller than the male, despite there being slightly more females of working age. The numbers of females in work or looking for employment (i.e. the female labour force) is only 70 per cent that of the male labour force. This is a consequence of norms and expectations both about child-rearing as well as notions of males as the principal bread-winners. It is, of course, exacerbated by poor provision of high-quality, affordable childcare.

Things could be different. The Eurostat Labour Force Survey (2000) showed that the Scandinavians take gender equality more seriously. The Danish rate of female employment was 72 per cent followed by Sweden with 69 per cent and Finland with 65 per cent. Ireland, at 51 per cent, was below the EU average of 53 per cent and ranked ninth of the 15 EU countries. The European Working Conditions Survey in 2000 found that 41 per cent of females spend an hour or more caring for children every day and 63 per cent do at least an hour of housework. The comparative figures for European males were 24 per cent and 12 per cent.

Female employment in Ireland is also paid less than male. A study entitled *How Unequal?* (published in 2000, edited by Callan et al.) calculated a sex "discrimination index" of about 15 per cent. Thus, women would earn 15 per cent more for their work, it is claimed, if they were men. This is apparent when the measure of pay per hour is compared (to control for the smaller number of paid hours of work that women do on average). In Figure 10.2 below, the differences in earnings per hour are displayed.

The gender gap, you will notice in Figure 10.2, is actually widening. In 1996, the difference was £2.16. By 2001, it was £2.47. Forget glass ceiling, this is a seven-pound-an-hour ceiling. Women's work also remains predominantly locked into a handful of stereotypical areas — three times as many women as men work in "education and health" and one-and-a-half times in "hotels and restaurants". Teaching, nursing, and waitressing are still the major career options for many women.

Figure 10.2: Male and Female Earnings in Pounds per Hour, All Industries (1996–2001)

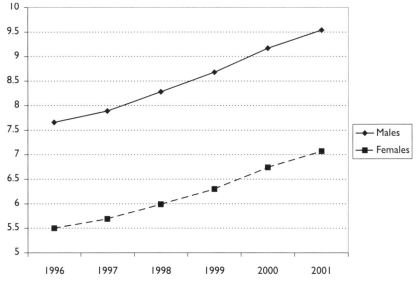

Source: CSO

Power Inequalities

Joy Rudd (1982) provided a review of the status of Irish women at the start of the 1980s. For the egalitarian, it made grim reading. Women were underrepresented in all elite areas and wherever important decisions were made. Rudd showed that women were marginalised, especially in higher grades of the civil service, in politics, in the labour force, in business and in government. She concluded:

> Irish women remain excluded from the main positions of formal power that control the society in which they live: women remain, at best, on the margins of the power elite. (p. 170)

There has been improvement since then — Mary Robinson's election was significant in many ways. However, the predominance of female candidates in the subsequent presidential election and the success of Mary McAleese cannot but support the suspicion that the presidency has become gendered in some strange way. Cosmetic hand-shaking, smiling and nodding is the job of the titular head of state while the real decisions are made on Kildare Street. And in government, there is a continued under-representation of women. There is a remarkable correspondence across Europe between gender imbalance in the general workforce and in government. Scandinavian societies — where women's roles are far less marginalised in the workplace and government — contrast sharply with societies like Ireland, Italy, Greece and Portugal where marginalisation in both is apparent. Figure 10.3 displays the percentage of women in ministerial positions (including ministers of state) across the EU.

Figure 10.3: Percentage Females in Government Positions in EU States in 2001

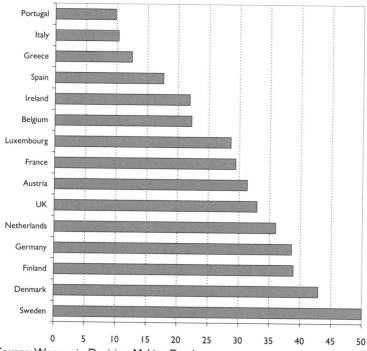

Source: Women in Decision-Making Database

The ministerial percentages in Figure 10.3 actually conceal even sharper bias. While women hold 22 per cent of ministerial positions in Ireland, they only comprise 13 per cent of current Dáil deputies. People spoke (somewhat disparagingly) of the "Blair Babes" after the Labour landslide in the UK in 1997 led to a large increase in the number of female MPs at Westminster. We still await the appearance of the Bertie Babes in Ireland.

There is an interesting relationship between post-materialist values in European societies and the position of women in politics (see Chapter 4 for a reminder of the meaning and definition of postmaterialism). When the percentages in Figure 10.3 are assessed in relation to the percentage of post-materialists by country as measured in the most recent relevant Eurobarometer, a strong positive relationship is revealed. Or in social science terms, there is a very strong correlation (of 0.72)[1] between these two sets of figures (see Table 10.1 for the raw data).

Table 10.1: Post-materialism and Female Political Power

	% Females in Government, 2001 (Women in Government database)	% Post-Materialists (Eurobarometer 1999)
Sweden	50.0	21.4
Denmark	42.9	25.8
Finland	38.9	14.2
Germany	38.6	15.0*
Netherlands	36.0	22.2
UK	32.9	14.0
Austria	31.3	9.3
France	29.4	21.8
Luxembourg	28.6	26.2
Belgium	22.2	12.6
Ireland	21.9	11.3
Spain	17.6	16.8
Greece	12.5	7.5
Italy	10.3	8.3
Portugal	9.8	6.9

Note: * Refers only to population in former West Germany.

Quite simply, post-materialism is more prevalent in societies with more female politicians. It is not likely that having more female politicians actually causes people to change their priorities towards greater post-materialism. What is more likely is that the type of so-

---

[1] The statistical strength of the relationship for the 15 cases or countries, with r = 0.72, is equal to 0.002 or would only occur by chance 1 in 500 times.

cieties which encourage and support women in developing political careers are also those societies where immediate short-term materialist goals are less common and where more advanced and sophisticated demands are prevalent. Ireland is not one of those societies.

In some respects, elaborate analyses are unnecessary in identifying sexism in Ireland. Conventionally, the Ministry of Finance is regarded as one of the most important government departments. The current ministerial incumbent is male, as is the Minister for State. So also are the Secretary General of the Department and the five Second Secretaries General. Only among the 12 Assistant Secretaries does a lone woman appear. At the Central Bank, the Director General, Deputy Director General, the five Assistant Directors General and 16 Heads of Function are male. In the IPA Yearbook for 2001, the judiciary section lists 125 judges of the Supreme Court, High Court, Circuit Court and District Court. Only 18 are women. And in academia, the presidents of Dublin City University, NUI Galway, NUI Maynooth, University College Cork, University College Dublin, University of Limerick, as well as the Provost of Trinity College Dublin are men. One of the hottest areas of growth in the last decade was the telecommunications industry. But only two of the top 12 management positions at Eircell are occupied by women. Of the 14 supervisory or board director positions at Eircom, one was held by a woman. Of the 15 top jobs in Esat, one woman was in place.

Gender, Perspective and Post-materialism

Thus, the formal position of women in Irish society is distinctly inferior to males, in easily demonstrable terms such as access to financial and power resources. While women have been drawn into the formal economy in increasing numbers, they remain disproportionally in part-time jobs, in less well paid employment and in certain typecast domains, and are systematically denied access to positions of power. In the UK, the McPherson report into the murder of the black teenager, Stephen Lawrence, described the Metropolitan Police as institutionally racist. Even the elementary sketch of statistics above demonstrates the presence of institutional sexism and inequality in Irish society. Taking account of that gender imbalance, can it be anticipated that women and men, by corollary, have different sets of political attitudes? For men, the last decade and a half have seen a great increase in income. For many women, these benefits are much more difficult to discern and can only be enjoyed indirectly through joint access to the male income. In the framework of post-materialist theory, therefore, there are good reasons to think that women and men might differ significantly. If the move away from materialist priorities and towards post-materialist ones is a function of personal wealth and security, and since it is patently obvious that women enjoy less of either in Ireland, then logically women should be less likely to select post-materialist priorities. In other words, a direct interpretation of the theory predicts sex differences. This is made more complex, though, by the fact that many married couples think of themselves as earning a single joint income — thus reducing the sharpness of inter-gender wealth comparisons. Furthermore, one aspect of post-materialism is a belief in the importance of equality as a goal in its own right. But for women, the belief in the importance of equality may reflect a desire for greater material equality rather than an abstract post-materialist belief. However, even if the predictability of gender differences in political attitudes is made a little foggier by these qualifications, they are hopefully a little more intriguing.

In an earlier chapter, differences in religious outlook among men and women were assessed. An interpretation of the figures suggested that women were slightly but consistently more religious than males. However, the decline in religiosity was at about the same rate for both genders. This does not contradict post-materialist expectations although too many explanations fit such a phenomenon for it to be utterly persuasive. What about a very "pure" post-materialist issue — the environment? How does gender impact upon ecological views? Unfortunately, no recent and direct replication of survey items is available. But indirect comparisons can be made between different surveys and they suggest that gender differences have a minor although unexpected influence. In 1993, the ISSP survey focused on attitudes to the environment. At this time, just before the years of intense economic growth, women were slightly but consistently less environmentally concerned than men were. For example, 43.7

per cent of Irish men agreed or strongly agreed that "they were worried that progress was harming the environment" while only 40.2 per cent of Irish women did. Of Irish males sampled, 57.7 per cent were either very or fairly unwilling to "cut their standards of living to protect the environment" while 61.1 per cent of females sampled fell into these categories. And 59.5 per cent of Irish males considered global warming to be extremely or very dangerous while 57.5 per cent of females did. In 1999, the Eurobarometer asked a different set of questions but also focused on the environment. On most of the items, females were now slightly more environmentally conscious. So, for example, 55.4 per cent of males sampled in Ireland considered environmental protection to be an immediate and urgent problem but 57.5 per cent of females did. About global warming, 70.8 per cent of men were very or somewhat worried but 73.5 per cent of women were. Women were more likely to be very or somewhat worried about the depletion of the ozone layer (82.3 per cent) than men (77.2 per cent) and were also more likely to be worried about the use of genetically modified components in food (74.0 per cent) than men (67.2 per cent).

This represents a move towards a slightly greater awareness or concern about ecological issues among women compared to men. In terms of the materialism/post-materialism divide, a sample of Irish males in a 1990 Eurobarometer survey showed lower levels of materialism than females (24.3 per cent of men compared to 28.5 per cent of women). By 1999, a later Eurobarometer was recording materialism levels of 25.8 per cent for males and 32.5 per cent for females. A favoured interpretation of this is that men's relative financial superiority has been strengthened by the boom and the faster growth of materialist priorities among women reflects their perceived comparative weakness in this regard. The gender differences, incidentally, in numbers opting for materialist priorities are mirrored across the EU, with a growth in materialist priorities among men but especially women throughout the 1990s.

There is evidence for growing disenchantment with politics, sharply evident among women and to a slightly lesser degree among men. The Eurobarometers in 1990 and 2000 asked people how often they discussed politics with friends. In 1990, about a quarter (25.2 per cent) of Irish men sampled said "never" against just over a third of women (37.3 per cent). By 2000, the equivalent levels were over a third of Irish males (37.0 per cent) compared to over half (50.8 per cent) the female sample. One occasionally hears worthy aspirations about making politics more interesting for young people. Might someone think about new forms of political discourse that are more women-friendly?

It may be the case that when surveys ask individuals their view on politics, people inevitably think of mainstream (or what radicals use to call "bourgeois") politics. Could these figures disguise perhaps the interest of both men and women in street politics? The ISSP surveys examined this issue in 1990 and 1996. The evidence in fact paints a fairly consistent picture in which Irish women were generally less favourable to alternative, radical or street politics than men were, and were even less so by 1996. For example, in 1990, 67 per cent of males and 58 per cent of females felt that, on occasion, one should follow one's conscience rather than the law. By 1996, the proportion of conscience-following females had dropped back to 56 per cent (and males to 65 per cent). Sixty per cent of males agreed in 1990 that public protest meetings definitely should be allowed, compared to 44 per cent of females. By 1996, the figures respectively were 56 per cent and 40 per cent. And women's support for the definite right to hold protest demonstrations (behind men's by about 13 per cent in both years) reduced from 36 per cent in 1990 to 32 per cent in 1996. About a fifth of women sampled in 1996 said they would definitely attend a demonstration or protest meeting if the issue was important, compared to a third of men. Politics, it seems, either in its dusty parliamentary format or (macho?) street protest mode, is increasingly a turnoff for men, but especially for women. Depending on your preferred political science theory, you may think that parliament is a waste of time and changes nothing, or alternatively you may think that demos and protests are a waste of time. However, the problem is that at least one of them may work, and if women in particular absent themselves from both avenues of action, then the current gender inequities will not be tackled wholeheartedly.

There have also been some interesting transfers of trust by men and women in different ways in popular institutions. The ISSP surveys of 1991 and 1998 asked individuals to express their levels of confidence in both business and industry as well as in churches and religious organisations. The percentages expressing either complete or a great deal of confidence in both institutions are presented in Figure 10.4 below.

Figure 10.4: Percentages of Irish Men and Women Expressing "Complete" or "A Great Deal" of Confidence in Business and Religious Institutions, 1991 and 1998

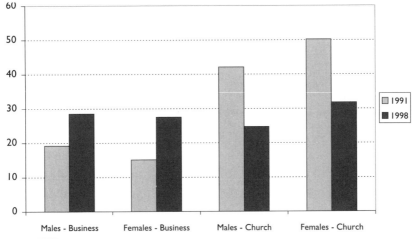

Source: ISSP

Put your faith in mammon, not God, was the clear lesson of the 1990s. At the beginning of the decade, men had more trust in business than women had and both genders had high levels of confidence in the church, especially women. The 1990s, though, seem to have witnessed a transfer of this confidence from church to business institutions. A loss of belief in the institution of religion does not necessarily mean a decline in spiritual or theistic beliefs. An argument made in an earlier chapter was that changes in actual religious belief are related more to factors of age, economic security and long-term secularisation forces. Figure 10.4, on the other hand, displaying the rapid transfer of confidence from one agency to another, is revealing the chickens coming home to roost in relation to *institutional trust*. It represents the dividend of high-profile media cases involving priests and abuse paralleled with the new gung-ho and can-do image of Irish business in the late 1990s.

Not surprisingly, given the national context of the 1990s with a thrusting resurgent business sector, as well as the international situation (where the disintegration of the USSR and its satellites demoralised and disorientated much of the Marxist and radical left), there was a decline in adherence to socialist thinking. What is surprising is how much sharper that decline was for women. The Eurobarometer in 1990 asked individuals to rate themselves on a left–right continuum and the gender differences were trivial (of Irish males sampled, 25.0 per cent placed themselves on the political left, as did 24.6 per cent of Irish females). However, by 1999, the same question found 16.8 per cent of men placing themselves politically on the left and only 10.8 per cent of women.

The decline of the left, especially among women, is confirmed by political polls. In 1995, the Eurobarometer asked people about their (first preference) voting intentions. Excluding the "don't know", "won't vote" and independent groups, 16.9 per cent of female respondents would have voted for one of Labour, Democratic Left or the Workers Party, compared to 20.3 per cent of males. Sinn Féin had the support of 3.4 per cent of males and 0.3 per cent of females. The Greens attracted 3.9 per cent of female voters and 3.1 per cent of males, while the respective percentages supporting the PDs were 2.8 per cent male and 2.6 per cent female. The two mainstream parties had the support of 70.3 per cent males and 76.1 per cent females (although polls usually appear to overestimate Fianna Fáil support relative to election performance). In total, the differences are not great, but men are slightly more likely to be "ideological" in their preferences while women have been drawn more towards the centre and centre-right parties in recent times.

Sexual Norms, Sexual Differences

As noted above and in previous chapters, the evidence suggests that women have been firmer adherents to religious values than men and slower to abandon those values. How has that impacted on views around sexual norms, about which traditionally the church has been vociferous? The pattern is not absolutely clear-cut, but comparative evidence from the 1991 and 1998 ISSP surveys suggests a few different patterns. In response to one question, towards sexual relations between same-sex adults, both men and women were strongly disapproving in 1991, with 67.0 per cent of Irish men and 68.6 per cent of women believing it was "always wrong". By 1998, there was a roughly equivalent (modest) liberalisation among both groups with 58.8 per cent of males and 60.7 per cent of females holding the view that it was always wrong.

In another question on sexual relations with someone other than one's spouse, a greater number of women were disapproving than men in surveys in 1991 and 1998. (Is it plausible to suggest that this may be related to gender differences in *actual* infidelity?) But there was a similar decline in numbers falling into the "always wrong" category between 1991 and 1998 — for women, it fell from 73.6 per cent to 65.8 per cent, while for men, the comparable percentages are 68.2 per cent and 60.2 per cent. The third pattern around sexual norms was that of differential change. In this case, it was related to sex before marriage and the proportion of men believing it was always wrong fell much more rapidly in the period of the two surveys (from 35.2 per cent to 24.0 per cent) than did women (from 37.0 per cent to 34.6 per cent). Finally, with regard to views on abortion, unfortunately the surveys did not pose identical or replicable questions at different times. In 1991, respondents were asked if the law should permit abortion if family income was very low. Among males, 60.1 per cent opted for "definitely not" against 67.8 per cent of females. In 1998, respondents were asked if a low-income family opting for abortion was wrong (there is thus a difference between the legal consideration to be made in the 1991 question and the moral consideration in 1998). "Always wrong" was the viewpoint of 56.7 per cent of Irish men sampled and 60.2 per cent of Irish women.

The Dying Phallus?

Much gender-related debate has been feminist-driven. This is hardly surprising given historical gender inequalities and the search for remedies. However, there has been a current of thought, influenced notably by new criminological perspectives on gender, which seeks to change the focus of debates. Instead of asking questions such as why women seem less successful in building careers in crime, theorists like Tony Jefferson have sought to investigate the link between masculinity and crime. Thus the stress is no longer on women's lower participation in offending but rather on why men are so heavily represented in crime statistics. This has generated one offshoot perspective on maleness that might be called the "end of men" hypothesis — a caricature version holds that men have become violent, academically poor, unable to nurture children and are increasingly maladjusted in information societies.

Anthony Clare recently published a popular book called *On Men: Masculinity in Crisis* where he argued that "at the beginning of the twenty-first century, it is difficult to avoid the conclusion that men are in serious trouble . . . anti-social behaviour is essentially male" (2000: 3). Most worryingly, for the average male chauvinist pig on the street, is women's growing assertiveness: "women are no longer prepared to be the property of patriarchal men" (p. 4). Clare's point is not that inequality and patriarchy are overthrown, but that their justification is in disarray. The traditional role of a man within the family and the duties and responsibilities of the father are no longer clear-cut, it is argued.

To a certain extent, the "end of men" hypothesis was a dramatic moral panic of the late 1990s. The growing dysfunctionality of a small segment of the male population in industrialised societies is of course worrying. But phrases like "the dying phallus", the "increasing redundancy of male violence", the "growing irrelevance of men to reproduction" and "the threat to the survival of men" (all of which appear in Clare's book) are overly catastrophist. In fact, the positive element should not be overlooked — if the rigid segregation of the past, whereby a successful or self-actualised man had to prioritise his career above all else and a successful or "proper" woman was above all a mother and housewife, can be overcome and its pervasive ideology rooted out for once and for all, then society must be a fairer and emotionally healthier place.

Show me the Mummy

Thus, attitudes about the working and domestic roles of women *and* men, held by women *and* men, are quite important, as is the direction in which they are changing. The most relevant data are provided by the ISSP surveys in 1988, 1991, 1994 and 1998. Tentatively, they seem to offer evidence for two phenomena, although this is merely my interpretation and others might easily read it differently. The more consistent finding is that men's attitudes persist in displaying greater amounts of social conservatism with regard to sex roles and equality. For example, when responding to items such as "what women really want is [*sic*] home and kids", "the household is a wife's job" and "housework satisfies as much as a paid job", the percentage of men in agreement or strong agreement is consistently greater than that of women. Typically, the difference is about ten per cent.

The second and more complex finding relates to change. Unfortunately, different questions are asked in the 1988 and 1994 surveys than in the 1991 and 1998 ones. This makes direct assessment impossible. However, the pattern seems to suggest that change was quite rapid among male and female respondents in their attitudes up to the beginning of the boom but that, since the mid-1990s, this change has eased off or even ceased. In other words, while a comparison between 1988 and 1994 shows rapid attitudinal movement among men and women, the differences between 1991 and 1998 are trivial or non-existent. In 1988, 61.9 per cent of males agreed that "what women really want is [*sic*] home and kids", as did 52.4 per cent of females. By 1994, the equivalent figures were 54.6 per cent of males and 47.6 per cent of females, about a 5–7 per cent shift for both sexes. On housework, around two-thirds (66.8 per cent) of men in 1988 agreed that it was as satisfying as other work compared to slightly fewer women (65.5 per cent). By 1994, the figures were 63.3 per cent for men and 59.4 per cent for women. And in response to the statement asking whether housework was the job of the wife, the percentage of assenting males declined between 1988 and 1994 from 46.4 per cent to 40.4 per cent, and females in the same period from 39.2 per cent to 29.0 per cent. However, the two items asked in the 1991 and 1998 surveys ("the husband's job is to earn money, the wife's job is to take care of the family" and "family life suffers if the woman works full-time") show changes of only about 1–2 per cent in that seven-year period. In summary, the neatest interpretation appears to be that, by the mid-1990s, a change had taken place whereby a large minority of men and a smaller minority of females still accepted the contours of traditional sex-roles (men as bread-winners, women in charge of home and children). However, this position did not fundamentally alter towards the end of the decade. There was one other relevant finding in the 1994 survey: when asked if family life suffered because *men* worked too much, 75 per cent of males and 76 per cent of females agreed. This should allay the fears of Clare that men's worth is in doubt — even in a traditionalist country like Ireland, both men and women recognise that family and home life suffers if men do not have a presence.

In Summary

What a typically male-authored chapter! It commences by acknowledging the subordination of women in Irish society and concludes by . . . worrying how men are getting on. At any rate, the overall substance of the chapter is as follows. Economic advance has meant that while women are better off in material terms, in relative terms (relative to men, that is), there has been no improvement. In the post-materialist framework, therefore, women might be expected to maintain more materialist values in comparison to males. By and large, this model was confirmed — women's support for post-materialist priorities has declined throughout the 1990s, apart from a small shift towards environmentalism. Politically, they have moved away from radical and critical ideologies. While, like men, their views have become more secularised and religio-sceptical, they continue to remain more sympathetic to the church than men. It was noted earlier, though, that in regards to equality and sex roles, women might be supportive from either a materialist (catching up with men) or post-materialist (the abstract notion of justice and fairness) perspective, or both. And certainly, it is a smallish minority of women who cling to the idea of rigid and outdated sex roles, while a larger and significant minority of Irish men do.

Chapter 11

DISTINCT WORLDS, DIVERGING VALUES

In the previous chapter, gender differences in attitudes were examined. In this chapter, there is a recognition that, just as Irish society is not homogeneous and can be viewed along separate gender lines, other divisions such as class and age must be assessed and understood. As we will see, these divisions are interesting in their own right as well as having a bearing on the future evolution of social values. Income is examined first, followed by age differences.

In a Class of Their Own

We don't like to think about class and class differences in Ireland. It runs counter to our self-concept as an essentially egalitarian nation, a society where rich and poor, or rather well off and not quite so well off, may freely mix, without elitism or "English"-style snobbery. "We're too small for classes", as a member of that rare breed, a self-declared Irish intellectual, supposedly once commented. Like so many of our other national conceits, this one is false. Ireland is one of the most economically unequal societies in Europe and has grown steadily more unfair in the recent past. Data gathered in interviews in 1993/94 and meticulously analysed by ESRI specialists Brian Nolan and Bertrand Maitre (published in 1999) show that the 12 EU member countries in 1993 could be divided into three camps with regard to equality. The egalitarian group consisted of the Netherlands, Den-

mark, Germany and Belgium.[1] The centrist grouping was composed of
Luxembourg, Italy, France and Spain. And the inegalitarian set was, and
is, made up of Ireland, the UK, Greece and Portugal. Thus, the richest
20 per cent of the population in countries like Ireland, Greece, the UK
or Portugal command a far greater proportion of income relative to
the bottom 20 per cent than in countries like Denmark and Germany.
(In the final chapter, the consequences of Ireland's choices in economic models and bedfellows are discussed in further detail).

Greece and Portugal at least have an excuse for their lack of
egalitarianism — they are poorer than Ireland and the UK, and there
is a moderate correspondence between overall poverty and inequality.[2] By corollary, wealthier societies in general tend to be fairer
ones (see Inglehart and Flanagan, 1987) but Ireland is proving a
mean-minded exception to this trend. The ESRI publication by Layte
et al. (2001) revealed, in yearly waves, increasing relative poverty in
Ireland between 1994 and 1998. The percentage of households falling below half the mean income line was 18.6 per cent in 1994. By
1998, it had risen to 24.6 per cent. Other societies have used their
growth to create more inclusiveness and fairness, while in Ireland, an
ever-expanding group of people are being muscled out of the party.
It might be protested that absolute poverty is declining — this point
was acknowledged in Chapter 3. But social psychologists have shown
that what matters to people, to their pride, their self-worth and
sense of justice . . . in other words, what is psychologically rather
than economically important, is relative, not absolute, deprivation
(see Walker and Pettigrew, 1984).

It is reasonable to anticipate, therefore, if social values are at least
partly determined by material and economic reality, that more than
most countries, Ireland will have a greater gulf in attitudes between
the richest and poorest, since the income gap is greater. However, as
was noted when assessing women's attitudes in the previous chapter,
the position of the poor may be complex *vis-à-vis* materialism and

[1] The subsequent accession to the EU in 1995 of Sweden, Finland, and Austria has increased the number of egalitarians, although the Norwegian decision not to join has
deprived the Community of one of the fairest societies in the world.

[2] A variant of Kuznets's Law in economics.

post-materialism. On the one hand, their subordinate financial position makes materialist priorities more urgent; on the other hand, their poor relative status means that equality, a post-materialist issue, should be valued more highly. In the analysis below, ISSP and Eurobarometer survey data are used to assess recent attitudes as well as those in the late 1980s and early 1990s. Where relevant comparisons are made with egalitarian societies, either Norway, which participated in most of the ISSP survey sweeps, or Denmark, which participated in the same Eurobarometer surveys as Ireland, are used. The sample of each country was divided into three according to income (lower, medium and high — by simply splitting the populations as near to the 33rd and 66th income percentile as possible).

There are sharp differences between the three income groups on the materialist/post-materialist index in Ireland. In the most recently available data (Eurobarometer 52.1) from 1999, the lowest income group emerge with a greater number of pure materialists. Of that group, 48.5 per cent are materialists in comparison to 18.7 per cent of the highest income third (with the middle-income group in an intermediary position — 28.3 per cent materialists). Those differences were far weaker earlier in the decade. In Eurobarometer 42 carried out in 1994, the comparative percentage of pure materialists among the high-income group was about the same at 19.6 per cent but for the low-income group, the figure was only 26.3 per cent. A coherent interpretation is that their worsening relative economic position over the 1990s has driven greater numbers of the poor towards materialist or scarcity priorities. In a far more egalitarian society like Denmark, the differences between income groups are far less — for example, among the poorest third of respondents in 1999, there were 14.7 per cent pure materialists and among the wealthiest, 3.9 per cent, a difference of only 10.8 per cent. The comparative difference in Ireland was 29.8 per cent (48.5 minus 18.7), almost three times as much. It may be argued that the Danes (and even more so the Norwegians, who are included in later analyses), like Scandinavian societies generally, show more collectivism and less individualism than Ireland. That is certainly true.[3] But the differences in the Irish context do not reflect greater individualism or whimsy — but rather the consistent and predictable determination of attitudes arising from marked economic inequalities among groups.

A similar pattern emerges when income groups are compared on frequency of political discussion. Eurobarometer 52 in 1999 posed this question and 17.0 per cent of the wealthiest third of respondents in Ireland said they frequently discussed politics with friends versus 10.6 per cent of the poorest third. A Danish comparison for 1999 shows a narrower difference between wealthiest and poorest thirds (respectively 22.2 per cent and 17.5 per cent). The ISSP surveys of 1996 and 1990 focused especially on attitudes to government and politics. As above, distinct differences between income groups in Ireland were found. In 1996, the highest income group was more favourable to "definitely allowing protest meetings" (57.6 per cent) and demonstrations (50.9 per cent) than was the lowest group — respectively 37.4 per cent and 35.6 per cent. In 1990, the same direction of effect had occurred but the discrepancy had not been so great in the earlier survey. (In 1990, 60.3 per cent of the higher income group were "definitely in favour of allowing protest meetings and 46.4 per cent definitely in favour of demonstrations while the respective figures for the lowest income group were 44.8 per cent and 34.1 per cent.) In Norway, income differences were associated with far smaller attitudinal discriminations. Of the poorest group in 1996, 71.2 per cent were definitely in favour of protests while 79.4 per cent of the richest third were. And for definite support for demonstrations, the figure were 58.2 per cent (among poorest) and 61.2 per cent (among wealthiest). Clearly, unconventional but important political values are influenced by income. And as income differentials have grown in Ireland, the attitude wedge has widened. More egalitarian societies, like Denmark and Norway, have smaller income distances between rich and poor and so post-materialist attitudes are more broadly shared.

---

[3] See Schwartz (1994) for a detailed discussion of cross-cultural research into dimensions of individualism and collectivism.

What about attitudes to more concrete and conventional political issues? With regard to the environment, there are predictable large discrepancies between income groups in Ireland. Eurobarometer 51.1 (carried out in 1999) examined people's ecological concerns in a general way and also specifically towards phenomena like global warming, the depletion of the ozone layer and genetically modified foods. What is interesting is the way in which income imprints itself so clearly onto the Irish data but not, for example, the Danish. So, while the difference between the percentage of high income (69.0 per cent) and low income Irish respondents (52.2 per cent) perceiving environmental protection to be an "urgent" problem was 16.8 per cent, the corresponding difference for Danish high (77.5 per cent) and low (67.3 per cent) income groups was only 10.2 per cent. Of high income Irish respondents, 45.1 per cent were very worried about global warming compared to 29.2 per cent of low income respondents, while in Denmark, slightly more *low* than high income respondents were very worried. Similarly, more *low* income Danes were concerned about ozone depletion and GM foods than were high income Danes. But in Ireland, more rigid income differences influence in turn more resolutely materialist priorities among the less well-off. The percentages reporting themselves as "very worried" about ozone depletion and GM foods among the less well-off were 38.9 per cent and 26.5 per cent while for the high-income group, the figures were 56.3 per cent and 50.0 per cent. Concern about the environment is a luxury that many of the poor cannot afford.

Race and racism have become hotter issues in Ireland. As was noted in a previous chapter, the post-materialist model predicts a positive relationship between increasing wealth and acceptance of new or "exotic" minorities. Unfortunately, there is no precise replication of attitudinal items over the 1990s and interpretation between different surveys must be employed. The 1995 ISSP survey focused on national identity and included questions dealing with attitudes to immigrants. The Irish sample displayed only minor differences at that time when income groups were compared. For example, 15.5 per cent of lower income respondents believed that the number of immigrants should be increased while 22.8 per cent of better-off respondents did. And 9.5 per cent of lower income respondents strongly agreed with the statement that immigrants take jobs away from people while 2.4 per cent of the top third of sample earners also agreed. In Eurobarometer 53, carried out five years later in 2000 (and following the first substantial flow of non-Irish immigration in the history of the state), a degree of change is noticeable, although a different set of questions was used. Of the less well-off, 22 per cent found the presence of people of different nationalities disturbing while 12.5 per cent of the well-off did. And the comparative figures of those "disturbed by the presence of people of other races" were 25.7 per cent and 14.2 per cent.

With regard to general trust in institutions, the gradual substitution of business for religion was noted in a previous chapter. In Figure 11.1, the proportions of rich and poor expressing "complete" or "a great deal" of confidence in business and religion are presented from the 1991 and 1998 ISSP surveys.

Figure 11.1: Confidence in Business and Religious Institutions among Rich and Poor, 1991 and 1998

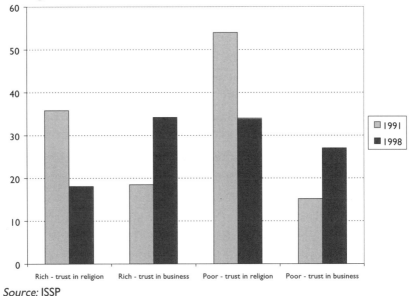

Source: ISSP

In Figure 11.1, the almost symmetrical transfer of trust from religion to business among better-off respondents is clear. While the less well-off have grown far more sceptical of religious institutions than previously, they have not worshipped our new financial gods with the same fervour as the better-off. Overall, though, the poor are more confident in the major institutions, as a single whole (religion and business), than the rich.

Attitudes towards sexual norms have evolved in the same way as political ones. In the ISSP surveys of 1991 and 1998, there is a consistent difference between the richest and poorest thirds of the Irish population with regard to items like sex before marriage, non-marital cohabitation, gay sex and extra-marital sex. Surprisingly, even towards items like "sex before marriage" the already considerable gulf in attitudes in 1991 (43.5 per cent of the low income group regarded it as "always wrong" compared to 24.8 per cent of the high income respondents) grew by 1998 when the respective figures were 38.7 per cent and 14.9 per cent. Thus, the divergence in 1991 was a substantial 18.7 per cent but by 1998, it had extended to 23.8 per cent. Overall, there is a growing liberalism on sexual matters among the Irish population, but the rate of change is far greater among the high-income group. On six measures related to sex, reproduction and childbirth, a comparison of well-off and less well-off Danes reveals trivial or no differences on five of the items. Only on attitudes to extra-marital sex was the gap between rich and poor substantial (and indeed greater than for the Irish groups).

With regard to sexual equality and participation in the workforce, there has been a stagnation of attitudes among the lowest income group. In 1991, 39.0 per cent of this group agreed or strongly agreed that it was the "husband's job to earn a wage and the wife's job to take care of the home" (versus 24.4 per cent of the high-income group). In 1998, 40.5 per cent of the low-income group took the same position (and 18.8 per cent of the high-income group). Similarly, in 1991 among low income respondents, 46.6 per cent agreed, or strongly agreed, that family life suffers if a mother works (and 35.9 per cent of the high income group). In 1998, the comparative figures were 48.7 per cent and 32.2 per cent.

The pattern is consistent across virtually all social attitudes. The growth of liberal and post-materialist attitudes is concentrated among the better off. But the poor, enduring the frustrations of ever more relative deprivation and injustice, are moving slowly, stabilising or even regressing back towards a hardened set of materialist, and socially conservative attitudes. These absolutist attitudes are a better social-psychological "fit" for an uncertain and difficult environment.

Finally, with regard to income, do different viewpoints exist toward poverty? In other words, do those who suffer the effects of harsh inequalities have noticeably different attitudes about inequality than those who do not? In terms of support for government priorities, it would appear so. The 1998 ISSP survey asked respondents whether governments should reduce the income gap between rich and poor. Among low-income respondents, 57.3 per cent believed that the government "definitely" should act to reduce inequalities. Support among the highest income respondents in the same survey, while significantly less, was still substantial, with 40.6 per cent agreeing that this definitely should be a government priority. (Thus, liberal conscience, or guilt, is not entirely extinguished among Ireland's better off.)

Although support for government action against inequality has increased among the poorest third (an earlier ISSP survey showed lower numbers in favour of wealth re-distribution),[4] an apparent paradox has been the steady decline of low-income respondents placing themselves politically on the left. The paradox is that wealth redistribution and equality are meant to be the classic concerns of the Left. Yet, in Eurobarometer 53 (2000), only 5.5 per cent of lower-income respondents placed themselves politically on the left (7 per cent if "Don't Knows" are taken account of). In 1995, the comparable figure was 17.5 per cent. Five years previously in 1990, it was 23.7 per cent. So while inequality has increased sharply over the decade and concerns about a government response have risen among the less well-off, the traditional left has failed to capture, indeed has lost this, their natural constituency. The stinging critique of the Labour Party leadership for its blandness and lack of commitment to social equality by Vincent Browne makes interesting reading in this regard ("Labour not convincing us at polls", *Irish Times*, 18 July 2001).

---

[4] In ISSP 1996, support among the poorest group of Irish respondents for government action to redistribute wealth was 28.6 per cent.

Young Ireland

Class (or income to be more precise) has an important impact on people's attitudes. But so too does age. You may recall some of those cringeworthy IDA advertisements in the 1980s where Ireland's youthful population was held aloft as a unique selling point to foreign investors. I was part of that youthful generation and, actually, we were fairly hideous en masse. But the feel-good ads did get it right about the sheer numbers of young Irish people in the population, at least prior to the annual waves of emigration. A very large birth rate meant that Ireland's demographic shape was quite distinct from our European counterparts. While this is changing rapidly, the bulge in Ireland's population is still located at a far younger age than is typical for the EU. The political leadership of countries like Germany is becoming increasingly worried about pension provision and finding the skilled workers to keep its economic powerhouse running. Ireland, on the other hand, faces into a period of serious growth in the number of self-conscious thirty-somethings. In Figure 11.2 below, the demographic profiles of the EU-15 and Ireland in 1998 are presented.

Figure 11.2: Age Profile of Irish and EU-15 Population in 1998

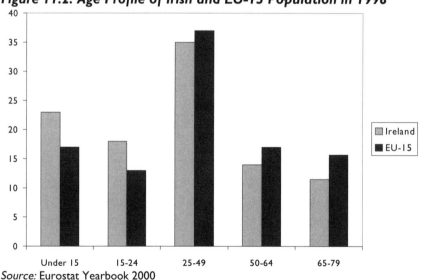

Source: Eurostat Yearbook 2000

As Figure 11.2 demonstrates, Ireland still has a relatively youthful population, with 41 per cent of its citizens under 25 compared to a 30 per cent EU average. And it's hackneyed but true — the young are our future. Their current and future attitudes are likely to be the social norms ten years from now and their disproportional size in the population makes it likely that their views will dominate to an even greater extent than elsewhere. Their psyche will be *the* Irish Psyche.

If, as was noted earlier, different income groups are living increasingly separate lives in Ireland (like Disraeli's notion of "the two nations, rich and poor"), then the young still more have a distinct set of experiences and core values. Ireland's long and ignoble tradition of economic failure, if they are even aware of it, has been passed on to them second hand, not directly experienced on the emigration boat. They are less religious than their parents or grandparents and if they have religious sentiment, it is cooler, less engaged than for youth in the past — as noted in Chapter 5, they probably prefer to think of it as "spirituality" rather than religion. The popularity of TV imports like *Friends* or watching one of Ireland's two favourite football teams (Man United and Anyone But United) on cable indicates just how permeated the lives of the young are with aspects of US and UK cultures. If young working people are spared the joblessness of the past, (at least at the time of writing) they do have in common their lower wages. Eurostat Yearbook 2000 provides mean earnings per hour for various age groups. Ireland's under-20-year-old workers receive less than a third of the earnings of 45–54 year olds and the 20–24 group less than half (only two EU countries out of the other 14 have age differentials anything resembling this).

Thus the young, apart from their distinctiveness in age, may have common issues as an economic grouping also. Does that mean they are more materialist in their attitudes than older people? The data point in the other direction, although modestly so. They suggest that young people's values may be shaped not just by their immediate economic environment but also by optimistic expectations of the future. And perhaps a certain youthful idealism is at work also. For example, in 1995, among the younger group (aged 17–30) of Irish respondents in the Eurobarometer survey, only 17.6 per cent fell into the "materialist" category in comparison with 24.5 per cent of those aged between 31 and 55 and 34.3 per cent of the older group (aged 56 and over). While a replication of these items in 1999 showed a slightly higher level of materialist values among the young (18.4 per cent), both of the older groups had a far greater increase in the proportion of materialists (29.1 per cent and 44.8 per cent).

In previous analyses, the issue of trust in institutions was also seen to be heavily influenced by gender and class identities. The same is partially true of age. There is little age impact, however, on degree of trust in business institutions. All three age groups (18–30, 31–55, 56+) in 1991 had low levels of trust in business, which rose steadily up to 1998. However, the loss of trust in religious organisations among the young is very clear over the same period. While in 1991, 34 per cent of young people had complete or a great deal of confidence in the church (compared to 21 per cent having confidence in business), by 1998, only 10.6 per cent had equivalent levels of confidence in the church (while those with confidence in business had risen to 28.8 per cent). Just as religious institutions were proving a turn-off for younger people, so too were political ones. Figure 11.3 presents the proportions of each age group who said they frequently or occasionally discussed politics. The sources are Eurobarometer surveys of 1990 and 1999.

Figure 11.3: Percentages of Different Age Groups who "Frequently or Occasionally" Discuss Politics, 1990 and 1999

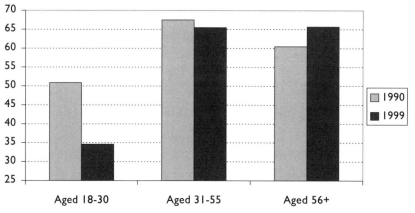

Source: Eurobarometer

The disaffection of the young with conventional politics is clear in Figure 11.3. What now happens to the energy once expended on politics is not clear. Voluntarism or charity work might be a suitable outlet for those who want to do something altruistic or socially helpful, but (and?) distrust politics. However, this area has not obviously benefited from youthful political scepticism — the ISSP survey of 1998 showed that 80.3 per cent of younger Irish respondents had been involved in no charitable activities in the previous twelve months. Participation in fact, was slightly higher among older respondents. Ruddle and Mulvihill's (1999) analysis of altruistic behaviour in Ireland showed that there was no increase in donations to charities in 1998 compared to 1994. On average, 39 per cent of survey respondents did some volunteer work for charities in 1992 but this slipped to 35 per cent overall in 1994 and 33 per cent by 1998. The middle-aged (those aged 40–59) gave significantly more of their time than did younger respondents (aged 20–39).

There are also significant age differences when one looks at belief in more radical political goals. However, the differences here are not between the under- and over-30-year-olds. If anything, respondents aged between 31 and 55 are more politically radical than their younger and older cohorts. In the 1996 ISSP survey, roughly two-thirds of younger and middle-aged respondents accepted that, in particular circumstances, one should obey one's conscience rather than the law, versus about half the older respondents. And 54.5 per cent of young and 54.3 per cent of the intermediate age group of respondents agreed, in the same survey, that public protests should definitely be allowed compared to only 30.4 per cent of those aged more than 55. Slightly more of the 31–55 age group said they would definitely attend a political protest or demonstration than the under-31s (and both were a lot more enthusiastic than the over-55s). In summary, the young, while slightly less driven by materialist priorities are not especially roused by an interest in either radical or conventional politics. Nor do they show any great signs of voluntarism or trust in religion. They are moving away by and large from all positions of ideological or practical commitment and are likely to prove poor targets for political parties looking for committed followers.

In left–right terms, young respondents curiously present the inverse pattern of the low-income group examined earlier. Those (low-income) respondents were more likely to be in favour of wealth redistribution than the better-off, but were less attracted by the political left, especially in recent years. The younger respondents (those aged thirty and less) on the other hand are somewhat *less* supportive than older ones of government action to reduce income disparities between the rich and poor but are *more* likely to place themselves on the political left than older respondents. It seems feasible, then, that the Left attracts them not because of its promise to redistribute wealth (since few people seem convinced the Irish Left can or will do this) but for other reasons — perhaps anti-authoritarianism, or secularism. For example, in the 1996 ISSP survey, only 35.3 per cent of younger respondents believed that the government should reduce income differences (versus 41.9 per cent of respondents aged 31–55 and 48.0 per cent of respondents over 55). And three-quarters of the youngest group in the same survey wanted tax cuts instead of more social services while only two-thirds of the older groups did. In Ireland, adhering to left-wing policies does not necessarily mean identifying with the political left — and vice versa.

Another paradox relates to ecological concerns. It can be argued that much of the Green agenda is long-term rather than short-term, or rather that green policies mean valuing the long-term welfare of the planet over short-term growth. On that basis, one would predict that older people, who are closer to death in actuarial terms, putting it bluntly, might be a little more cavalier about green issues. But the opposite is true. The Eurobarometer survey in 1999 on the environment showed that, on average, older Irish respondents were more worried about issues like global warming, ozone depletion and GM foods than were the younger cohort.

With regard to concrete political issues, only on items related to immigration are the young clearly more post-materialist than older people are. In the ISSP survey of 1995, younger respondents were less likely to "strongly agree that immigrants take jobs from Irish people" than were older ones. And in the 2000 Eurobarometer, far fewer of those aged 30 and under said they were disturbed by the presence and customs of those from other countries (11.8 per cent) than those aged between 31 and 55 (14.9 per cent) and those aged 56 and over (23.7 per cent). When asked if they were disturbed by the presence of people of another race, the corresponding figures were 13.6 per cent for the young, 17.9 per cent for the intermediate age group and 27.6 per cent for the older group.

The area in which the greatest age distinctions were clearest related to sexual norms and roles. It is in this domain that the young and old in Ireland live in different communities, quite simply, each with their own value systems. It is true that, even before the 1990s, the young tended to be far less conservative on sexual matters, but the last decade saw the split widen further between them and their older counterparts. The term "partner" (a bit like expensive bottled water, in that nobody could quite believe it would gain popularity here) is starting to achieve wide currency, especially among younger people, and this reflects something of their new sets of attitudes. The ISSP survey items which permit comparison of responses in 1998 with those of 1994, 1991 and 1988, unambiguously chart the march of change among young people. The difference between 1988 and 1994 is modest but becomes very rapid when the comparison is extended to 1998. So for example, back in 1988, we find that 37.4 per cent of young people — those aged 18–30 — agreed (including "strongly agreed") that the family suffers when a mother works. Of older respondents (over 55), 72.9 per cent were in agreement. In both cases, there was a minor decline when these survey items were replicated six years later and agreement of young people had declined to 33.6 per cent (and among older respondents, 69.9 per cent). Similarly in that 1988–1994 period, modest moves away from traditionalism were apparent for younger and older groups for agreement with the claim that "women really want home and kids" (change from 43.1 per cent to 32.6 per cent among younger people) and "household work satisfies as much as a paid job" (56.5 per cent to 47.3 per cent among the young).

But it is the changes recorded up to 1998 that are the most remarkable. The percentage of young people agreeing that the family suffers when a mother works was 37.4 per cent in 1988, as was noted above. By 1998, the proportion of young people agreeing with the same statement had halved to 19.5 per cent. Older respondents supporting the statement had also declined, but not as steeply (from 72.9 per cent to 62.0 per cent).

On attitudes towards sexual behaviour, the changes between 1991 and 1998 were also remarkable. Figure 11.4 below traces the movement of views among three age groups towards pre-marital, extra-marital and gay sexual relations.

Figure 11.4: Percentage of Age Groups Believing Three Sexual Behaviours to be Wrong, 1991 and 1998

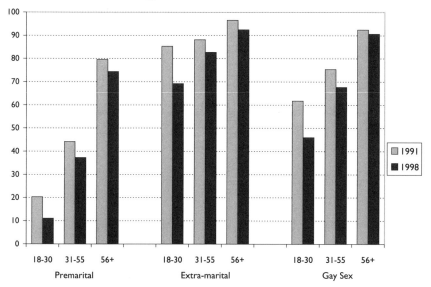

Source: ISSP

Figure 11.4 reveals both a phenomenal age-differentiation in relation to sexual attitudes as well as tremendous change among the younger respondents over time. And it must be remembered that the time span involved is only seven years, not much more than the gap between two general elections.

On attitudes to abortion among the young, some changes should also be noted. In ISSP 1991, 31.0 per cent of younger respondents believed that the law should allow a woman to obtain an abortion or termination if the baby potentially had a serious medical defect. Of the intermediate age group, 27.2 per cent agreed, as did 16.3 per cent of the older respondents. Again in seven short years, a rapid shift has occurred.[5] In 1998, 40.2 per cent of younger respondents believed that termination where the baby potentially had a serious medical defect was "not wrong at all" (and a further 26.3 per cent thought it was "wrong only sometimes").

Overall, it is clear that attitudes, and attitude change, are not evenly distributed among different income and age groups in Ireland. Rather, social class and age clearly imprint themselves on values and outlook. The lower income group have been in relative economic decline in Ireland and there is some evidence for a retreat towards defensive materialist attitudes. The younger group are slightly different and their views might be described as having an impetus towards freedom or liberation. This is an important claim and will be taken up in the concluding chapter.

---

[5] Although as noted in the previous chapter, the use of slightly different wording makes direct comparison problematic.

Chapter 12

THE NEW IRISH PSYCHE

There is a spectre haunting Ireland — the spectre of individualism. The largely unexpected economic explosion of the 1990s, up to its peak in late 2000, offered tremendous opportunities to this society. And most of those opportunities have been spurned. The data gathered in this book permit a calculation of the balance sheet of Irish economic growth, through the framework of post-materialism. We have seen that certain limited expectations of a post-materialising society have been realised. There has been a move away from religious dogma, a degree of pluralism with regard to people's private lives, a growing recognition that sexuality does not have to be compressed into one model for all people and a slow realisation that traditional gender roles were deeply oppressive to women, and in fact to men as well. But is that really good enough? And is it really "post-materialist"? In fact, the changes that have occurred in Ireland only partially match the post-materialist hypothesis. Is there any consistent evidence of a new and innovative radicalism in the political world? The demand for widespread social equality is, if anything, weaker than in the past. Have quality of life or cultural issues been placed on the national agenda? Not at all. Is public discourse enriched? In no obvious way. The changes might be better described as brutal modernisation, with rampant consumerism and individualism leading the charge.

The historian Isaac Deutscher once spoke of the three tragedies or problems that have always beset our species: food, sex and death.[1] As a Marxist, he believed that socialism could deal with the first of these problems, material want. Humans would still have the other two matters with which to concern themselves, but at least with material want out of the way, they would be in a better position to do so. In a less dramatic way, the boom of the 1990s enabled Irish society to transcend, or at least suspend, the traditional worries of unemployment and emigration that hitherto created such misery. The window of opportunity was there to go beyond these materialist concerns and really raise the level of Irish culture. The main aim of this book has been to examine the shifts in attitude and values of Irish people as a consequence, in the intervening period. In this way, and returning to the question posed earlier, what has our wealth actually done to us, or for us? In Chapter 4, Positive and Negative Views of wealth were contrasted. The Positive View proposed that sustained economic growth and financial security enable a society to go beyond simple materialism towards better self-expression, abstract concerns about democracy and equality, quality of life issues such as the nature of our cities and environment and a rejection of absolutism. In the Negative View, materialism generates a further cycle of materialism, consumerism, individualism, money as an end-in-itself, and political priorities favouring personal gain over public good.

It appears that the balance sheet, at least based on the evidence presented here, is that, although minor elements of the Positive View were sustained, the Negative View is a better general model of change in Ireland. The last decade had great potential to enrich the systems of education, arts, culture in its narrow and broad senses, politics, equality and social support. But advances were meagre. It seems to me that the attitudes of the young, examined in the latter half of the previous chapter, really capture the essence of the changes that did take place. And these can be encapsulated as a race for freedom. "Freedom" of course generally has positive connotations and in some ways, at least from a liberal perspective, the race

---

[1] In his essay *On Socialist Man*, published in 1967. In fact he was paraphrasing the ideas of the revolutionary, Leon Trotsky.

for freedom was a positive one — away from the claustrophobic constraints of the old society, crushing poverty, a psychological sense of failure and post-colonial attitudes. It also meant emancipation from a domineering and often cruel church as well as more liberty in deciding how individuals want to live their lives. New sexual freedoms, and the right to remarry as well as more choices about alternative lifestyles have been progressive.

But the race for freedom has also meant a race away from certain duties — duties around fairness to vulnerable sections of society, obligations to help others, the need to bring everyone else along. As soon as we broke the shackles of poverty, we dashed towards consumerism. We have escaped the choking grasp of the church but in so doing have also abandoned the positive pro-social element of its message. This is the negative element of freedom — voracious individualism that pushes all else to one side. Forget about pollution and congestion; I need a car. It doesn't matter about the poor; I need a tax break. Too bad about the needs of the community; I don't have the time. Some constraints of the past certainly needed to go. But that did not mean all social constraints and responsibilities were bad.

In a recently published book, a colleague of mine, Ciaran Benson (2001) has analogised modern life as a navigation of the self, finding one's way in the world. In a wider way, we can think of social development as a journey. In what direction is the Irish Psyche travelling? Where is its ultimate destination? Those changes of substance that have occurred, and been identified in this text, have been explosive. And if the rate of change continues as it has done, the New Irish Psyche will be a hyper-individualistic one, dominated by rampant consumerism. It will exist in a society where people know the price of everything but, increasingly, the value of nothing. And individuals will insist that they must be free — free from want but also free from obligation.

However, sociological journeys are hard to predict. Change does not always occur along a simple linear path and both qualitative and quantitative shifts may occur. In extrapolating from the present, two possible scenarios present themselves as models of future development.

Scenario One — Be Patient

It may be that individualism and consumerism are only temporary responses to the poverty of old. Thinking about the post-materialist hypothesis once more, it is clear that central in social-psychological significance is the feeling of security that economic growth brings. And yet there must be some uncertainty over the temporal nature of psychological security. If people have known consistent poverty for many years, and then experience new levels of wealth, it must take time to be reassured it's there to stay. And for much of the 1990s, Irish people did view the boom with a somewhat disbelieving air. It took a lot of convincing that it was actually happening. It is no longer so surprising, but the idea for example that people would *want* to immigrate to *this* country was, even in the mid-1990s, quite hard to believe, as was the notion that we would have to deal with the problems of success.

If one looks at the rise of post-materialism in Germany, it did not appear as a serious force until the student radicalism of the late 1960s and the Green movement of the 1970s. Yet spectacular economic recovery and growth actually occurred much earlier, in the 1950s and early 1960s (see Urwin, 1989). Similarly, Italy's often overlooked economic *miracolo*, with growth rates almost as dramatic as those of Germany, also occurred prior to the mid-1960s, yet the post-materialism of ultra-leftism, direct action, as well as the "hot summer" and "hot autumn" political strikes occurred in the late 1960s and 1970s. In other words, it took many years before the psychological security provided by rapid economic growth transformed values and beliefs. In fact, even after it was wrongly, but widely, accepted in the mid-1960s industrialised world that recessions were a thing of the past, post-materialist values did not automatically appear.

It may be that Ireland will require more time and reassurance that the bad old days will not return before significant value and cultural shifts occur. And more years of steady growth are probably also required. It is possible that after the initial, almost panicked rush towards consumerism, we may be able to become more relaxed and thoughtful about our wealth. We hungered for the trappings of money for a long time — now that we have them, we may be able to gradually look up from our plates. Perhaps the first signs of this are in the debate over the health service. We saw in Chapter 8 how it has declined despite the conditions of plenty prevailing. But there are now far-reaching plans afoot in the current Health Strategy that should increase numbers of consultants, nurses and hospital beds, as well as reorganising the entire health structure. This will cost a huge amount of money but appears to be favoured by taxpayers and politicians alike.

The only problem, if this post-materialist and anti-individualist sign is valid, is that of time — we may have run out of it. A hard recession grows ever more likely. Economic clouds have gathered, and job losses are becoming more frequent. In Figure 12.1 below, the number of times the phrase "economic slowdown" has appeared in *The Irish Times* over an 18-month period are graphed. The direction is obvious (and the headlines were not of the "No Economic Slowdown Expected" kind). It may be that, just when people were beginning to grow accustomed to a new environment, it will be swept away as the US economy goes into recession and takes Ireland with it.

Figure 12.1: Number of References to "Economic Slowdown" in **The Irish Times** *over an 18-month Period*

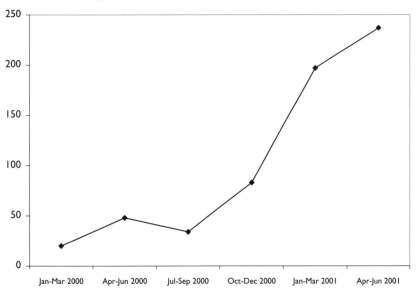

The spectacular atrocities in the US on 11 September 2001 must also have an impact beyond even the horrendous numbers directly killed by the attacks. The climate of post-materialism — internationalism, a liking for the new and different, a belief in human rights and individual liberties as well as a desire for globalisation in the best sense of the word — will be challenged by suspicion, xenophobia, militarism and chauvinism. Fear and loathing in New York echo around the world and further constrict international trade and travel, the oxygen of economic growth. And this New World Disorder promises to endure. Americans and their allies witnessed an act of incomprehensible cruelty, unspeakable savagery and immeasurable horror. They seek to construct a global coalition to crush the fanatics and those who slyly harbour or support them. In the Muslim world, on the other hand, the unpalatable reality is that very many people hold the US directly or indirectly responsible for the half-a-million Iraqi children who have died because of UN sanctions, the continuing torment and occupation of Palestine as well as Clinton's arguably pretext-less bombing of a Sudanese pharmaceutical plant. Thus, in their view, the attacks represented a taste of its own medicine for an arrogant and brutal superpower. The two worldviews — those of a wounded North and a long suffering South — are probably further apart than even those of the USA and USSR at the height of the Cold War. The horror show will run and run.

This scenario is a bleak one. The uncomfortable news, though, is there is a likelier and perhaps gloomier possibility, whereby Irish society is not undone primarily by world events but by its own nature and dynamics.

Scenario Two: Anglo-Saxon Attitudes?

In Chapters 7 and 11, the growing inequalities of Irish society were described. The detailed work by researchers at the ESRI has confirmed not only that Ireland is one of the most unequal societies in the EU but that it is growing ever more so. At the end of July 2001, CORI's Justice Commission published figures showing that the most recent budgets continued to add to inequalities in Irish society. Earlier that month, an *Irish Times* editorial quoted J.K. Galbraith:

as people become fortunate in their personal well-being, and
as countries become similarly fortunate, there is a common
tendency to ignore the poor.

Wealth giving rise to inequality is possible. But it doesn't have to be
that way. There are societies where wealth and high levels of social
equality very comfortably co-exist. And then there are societies
where they run counter to each other. The US and, in recent years,
the UK are examples of the latter sort. Ireland looks increasingly
more like these societies, in its wealth and cruel inequalities. Naturally, psyche and attitudes must also adapt to the new reality.

Let's take the US as the ideal type or embodiment of these societies. It is a remarkably "free" society in economic terms. Absent are
the heavy social market costs that offer some protection to the
workers in the EU. Taxation is relatively low (although still considerable). It is a winner-take-all kind of free society where those who are
doing well can experience remarkably enhanced lifestyles. But if you
lose, you lose access to all possibility of quality services — in education, health, social support.

> There is little spending on social welfare and levels of corpo-
> rate and personal taxation are low. Welfare entitlements are
> tightly monitored and means-tested; social security contribu-
> tions are at the lower end of the international scale. (Hutton,
> 1995: 258)

This is an economy which can produce a huge number of jobs very
quickly, "although by European standards they are astonishingly
poorly paid, with the bottom tenth of the workforce earning 38 per
cent of median earnings" compared to 67 per cent in the EU
(Hutton, ibid.). It is characterised by its critics as generating the
"promotion of consumption over long-term investment, systematic
inequality and lack of social provision" (Hutton, 1995: 259). The
business cycle is fast and merciless — think of the aggressive action
of Alan Greenspan and the Federal Reserve on interest rates versus
the slow and gentle tinkerings of the European Central Bank. Production and jobs come and go very quickly. According to Hutton,
one in five US workers expects to lose his or her job within the next

year and another 20 per cent expect periods of unemployment. Thus, the US sporadically displays impressive growth but without long-term security for many working people.

Ireland seems more and more drawn to this type of society and its obsessive individualism, its hostility to taxation, its exuberant freedom — all at a price. A substantial section of the Irish political elite strains to join the "boom and bust" group of Anglo-American economies. Their mantra is freedom through the market. The absence of a strong social-democratic tradition in Ireland means that intellectual opposition to the mantra is muted. The shorthand "Boston or Berlin", is a useful phrase with which to contrast the Anglo-American world, where finance is largely unbound, versus social market Europe where the state or public still provides, in many societies, quality education and health free at the point of delivery. In social market Europe, inclusiveness and quality of life are not always runners-up, subordinated to the rights of unbridled profit.

Ireland has moved away from Berlin, or perhaps we should say Stockholm, in the last decade, and towards Boston. The problem for attitudes and values is that security and stability are precisely the kinds of things that cannot be provided by the Boston model. People must continue to remain vigilant in those societies. You can smile when you're winning but if things go wrong, then they go very badly wrong. In a winner-take-all society, one can never overlook the possibility or threat of unemployment or unexpected hardship. Thus, one can never ignore the materialist imperative. For real change to occur in people's values, economic growth is important but just as important is the *context* and *manner* in which the growth occurs. Without the guarantee of security and fairness, our values will be overshadowed by fear and materialist obsession. Under those circumstances, the Irish psyche will experience change, but not transformation.

REFERENCES

Adorno, T.W. (ed.) (1950), *The Authoritarian Personality*, New York: Harper & Bros.

Allen, Kieran (2000), *The Celtic Tiger: The Myth of Social Partnership in Ireland*, Manchester: Manchester University Press.

Ardagh, J. (1995), *Ireland and the Irish: Portrait of a Changing Society*, Harmondsworth: Penguin.

Arts Council of Ireland (1999), *The Arts Plan 1999–2001: A Plan for Government, A Strategic Framework for the Arts*, Dublin: The Arts Council.

Arts Council of Ireland (various years), *Annual Report*, Dublin.

Banks, L.R. (1960), *The L-Shaped Room*, London: Chatto and Windus.

Barnes, J. (1998), *England, England*, London: Jonathan Cape.

Benson, C. (2001), *The Cultural Psychology of Self: Place, Morality and Art in Human Worlds*, London: Routledge.

Breen R. (ed.) (1990), *Understanding Contemporary Ireland: State, Class and Development in the Republic*, Dublin: Gill & Macmillan.

Brody, H. (1973), *Inishkillane: Change and Decline in the West of Ireland*, London: Allen Lane.

Browne, V. (2001), "Labour not convincing us at polls", *Irish Times*, 18 July.

Callan, T. (ed.) (2000), *How Unequal? Men and Women in the Irish Labour Market*, Dublin: Oak Tree Press.

Casey, S. and O'Connell, M. (2000), "Pain and Prejudice: Assessing the Experience of Racism in Ireland" in M. MacLachlan and M. O'Connell (eds.), *Cultivating Pluralism: Psychological, Social and Cultural Perspectives on a Changing Ireland*, Dublin: Oak Tree Press.

Central Statistics Office data obtained from CSO website at http://www.cso.ie.

Central Statistics Office (2000), *National Income and Expenditure*, Dublin: Stationery Office.

Central Intelligence Agency (2000), *World Factbook 2000*, www.cia.gov/cia/publications/factbook/index.html.

Clare, A. (2000), *On Men: Masculinity in Crisis*, London: Chatto & Windus.

Coogan, T.P. (1987), *Disillusioned Decades: Ireland 1966–87*, Dublin: Gill and Macmillan.

CORI Justice Commission (2001), "Ireland's poorest betrayed by government as rich/poor gap widens even further", Press Release, www.cori.ie/justice/news_releases, 23 July.

Crotty, R. (1966), *Irish Agricultural Production*, Cork: Mercier Press.

Crotty, W. and Schmitt, D.E. (eds.) (1998), *Ireland and the Politics of Change*, London: Longman.

Curry, P. (2000), "'She never let them in . . .': Popular Reactions to Refugees Arriving in Dublin" in M. MacLachlan and M. O'Connell (eds.), *Cultivating Pluralism: Psychological, Social and Cultural Perspectives on a Changing Ireland*, Dublin: Oak Tree Press.

Dangerfield, G. (1935), *The Strange Death of Liberal England*, London: Random House.

Davies, N. (1999), *The Isles: A History*, London: Macmillan.

De la Fuente, A. and Vives, X. (1997), "The Sources of Irish Growth" in A.W. Gray (ed.), *International Perspectives on the Irish Economy*, Dublin: Indecon.

Department of Education (1995), *Charting our Education Future* (White paper on education), Dublin: Stationery Office.

Deutscher, I. (1954), *The Prophet Armed: Trotsky 1879–1921*, Oxford: Oxford University Press.

Deutscher, I. (1967), *On Socialist Man* (Address to the second annual Socialist Scholars Conference, 1966), New York: Merit Publishers.

Elias, N. (1978), *The Civilising Process* (Vol. 1), Oxford: Basil Blackwell.

EU Employment and Social Affairs (2001), *Women in Decision-Making Database*, www.db-decision.de/index.html.

Euromonitor data – drawn from the *Global Market information Database*, gmid@euromonitor.com.

European Commission (various years), *Eurobarometer Survey Series*, Luxembourg: European Commission.

Eurostat (2000), *A Statistical Eye on Europe: Data 1988-98* (Eurostat Yearbook 2000), Luxembourg: Office for Official Publications.

Eurostat (2000), *Key Data on Health 2000*, Luxembourg: Office for Official Publications.

Eurostat (2000), *Labour Force Survey*, Luxembourg: Office for Official Publications.

Fahey, Tony (1992), "Catholicism in Ireland" in P. Clancy (ed.), *Ireland and Poland: Comparative Perspectives*, Dublin: Department of Sociology, University College Dublin.

Fanon, F. (1968), *The Wretched of the Earth*, New York: Grove Press.

Gaffney, M. (1996), *The Way We Live Now*, Dublin: Gill and Macmillan.

Galbraith, J.K. (1985), *The Affluent Society* (4th ed.), London: Deutsch. (1st edition 1958; 2nd edition 1969)

Galbraith, J.K. (1992), *The Culture of Contentment*, London: Sinclair-Stevenson.

Galbraith, J.K. (1999), *Name-dropping, from F.D.R. On*, Boston: Houghton Mifflin.

Gibbons, L. (1996), *Transformations in Irish Culture*, Cork: Cork University Press.

Ginsborg, P. (1990), *A History of Contemporary Italy: Society and Politics 1943–1988*, London: Penguin.

Greeley, A.M. and Ward, C.W. (2000), "How 'secularised' is the Ireland we live in?", *Doctrine and Life*, Vol. 50, pp. 581–617.

Hobsbawm, E.J. (1994), *The Age of Extremes: The Short Twentieth Century, 1914–1991*, London: Michael Joseph.

Houghton, J. (1998), "The Dynamics of Economic Change" in W. Crotty and D.E. Schmitt (eds.), *Ireland and the Politics of Change*, London: Longman.

Hourihane, A.M. (2000), *She Moves Through the Boom*, Dublin: Sitric Books.

Hussey, G. (1993), *Ireland Today: Anatomy of a Changing State*, Dublin: Town House.

Hutton, W. (1995), *The State We're In*, London: Jonathan Cape.

Indecon International Economic Consultants in association with PriceWaterhouse Coopers (1999), *Succeeding Better: Report of the Strategic Review of the Arts Plan 1995–1998*, Dublin: Stationery Office.

Inglehart, R. (1990), *Culture Shift in Advanced Industrial Society*, Princeton, N.J.: Princeton University Press.

Inglehart, R. (1997), *Modernization and Postmodernization: Cultural, Economic, and Political Change in 43 Countries*, Princeton, NJ: Princeton University Press.

Inglehart, R. (1977), *The Silent Revolution: Changing Values and Political Styles among Western Publics*, Princeton, NJ: Princeton University Press.

Inglehart, R. and Flanagan, S. (1987), "Value Change in Industrial Societies", *American Political Science Review*, Vol. 81, pp. 1289–1319.

Inglis, T. (1987), *Moral Monopoly: The Catholic Church in Modern Irish Society*, Dublin: Gill and Macmillan.

Inglis, T. (1998), *Moral Monopoly: The Rise and Fall of the Catholic Church in Modern Ireland*. Dublin: University College Dublin Press.

Institute of Public Administration (2001), *IPA Yearbook 2001*, Dublin: IPA.

Irish Universities Nutrition Alliance (2001), *North/South Ireland Food Consumption Survey*, Dublin: Food Safety Promotion Board.

ISSP (1986–1998), *International Social Survey Programme*, Cologne: Zentralarchiv für Empirische Sozialforschung.

Kenny, V. (1985), "The Post-colonial Personality", *Crane Bag*, Vol. 9, pp. 70–78.

Kerrigan, G. and Brennan, P. (1999), *This Great Little Nation: The A-Z of Irish Scandals & Controversies*, Dublin: Gill and Macmillan.

Kiberd, D. and Longley, E. (2001), *Multiculturalism: The View from the Two Irelands*, Cork: Cork University Press.

Klein, N. (2000), *No Logo: No Space, No Choice, No Jobs, Taking Aim at the Brand Bullies*, London: Flamingo.

Lane, R.E. (2000), *The Loss of Happiness in Market Democracies*, New Haven: Yale University Press.

Layte, R., Maître, B., Nolan, B., Watson, D., Whelan, C.T., Williams, J. and Casey, B. (2001), *Monitoring Poverty Trends and Exploring Poverty Dynamics in Ireland*, Policy Research Series (PRS) No. 41, Dublin: Economic and Social Research Institute.

Lee, J. (1989), *Ireland 1912–1985: Politics and Society*, Cambridge: Cambridge University Press.

Levi, P. (1988), *The Drowned and the Saved*, London: Joseph.

Lukes, S. (1974), *Power: A Radical View*, London: Macmillan.

MacSharry, R. and White, P. (2000), *The Making of the Celtic Tiger: The Inside Story of Ireland's Boom Economy*, Cork: Mercier.

Maslow, A.H. (1954/1970), *Motivation and Personality*, (2nd ed.), New York: Harper and Row.

McDonald, F. (2000), *The Construction of Dublin*, Kinsale: Gandon Editions.

Mintel Market Research Reports, supplied by *Mintel Services*, part of Mintel International Group, Mintel.com.

Moane, G. (1994), "A Psychological Analysis of Colonialism in an Irish Context", *Irish Journal of Psychology*, Vol. 15, pp. 250–265.

National Economic and Social Council (1993), *Education and Training Policies for Economic and Social Development*, Report No. 95, 1993.

Nic Ghiolla Phádraig, M. (1986), "Religious Practice and Secularisation" in P. Clancy, S. Drudy, K. Lynch and L. O'Dowd (eds.), *Ireland: A Sociological Profile*, Dublin: Institute of Public Administration.

Nic Ghiolla Phádraig, M. (1995), "The Power of the Catholic Church in the Republic of Ireland" in P. Clancy, S. Drudy, K. Lynch and L. O'Dowd (eds.), *Irish Society: Sociological Perspectives*, Dublin: Institute of Public Administration / Sociological Association of Ireland.

Nolan, B. and Maître, B. (1999), *The Distribution of Income Poverty in the European Community Household Panel*, ESRI working paper No. 107, Dublin: Economic and Social Research Institute.

O'Connell, P. and Lyons, M. (1995), *Enterprise-related Training and State Policy in Ireland: The Training Support Scheme* (ESRI Policy Research Series, No. 25), Dublin: The Economic and Social Research Institute.

O'Hearn, D. (1998), *Inside the Celtic Tiger*, London: Pluto Press.

Organisation for Economic Co-operation and Development (2000), *Education at a Glance*, Paris: OECD.

O'Toole, F. (1995), *Meanwhile Back at the Ranch: The Politics of Irish Beef*, London: Vintage.

Paxman, J. (1998), *The English: A Portrait of a People*, London: Michael Joseph.

Peillon, M. and Slater, E. (eds.) (1998), *Encounters with Modern Ireland: A Sociological Profile, 1995–1996*, Dublin: Institute of Public Administration.

Peillon, M. and Slater, E. (eds.) (2000), *Memories of the Present: A Sociological Chronicle, 1997–1998*, Dublin: Institute of Public Administration.

Reed, J. (1966), *Ten Days that Shook the World*, Harmondsworth: Penguin.

Rudd, J. (1982), "On the Margins of the Power Elite: Women in the Upper Echelons" in M. Kelly, L. O'Dowd and J. Wickham (eds.) *Power, Conflict and Inequality*, Turoe Press: Dublin.

Ruddle, H. and Mulvihill, R. (1999), *Reaching Out: Charitable Giving and Volunteering in the Republic of Ireland. The 1997/98 Survey*, Dublin: Policy Research Centre.

Schwartz, S.H. (1994), "Beyond Individualism–Collectivism: New Cultural Dimensions of Values" in U. Kim, H.C. Triandis, C. Kagitcibasi, S. Choi and G. Yoon (eds.), *Individualism and Collectivism: Theory, Method, and Applications. Cross Cultural Research and Methodology*, 18.

Sweeney, A. (1999), *Irrational Exuberance: The Myth of the Celtic Tiger*, Dublin: Blackhall.

Sweeney, P. (1998), *The Celtic Tiger: Ireland's Economic Miracle Explained*, Dublin: Oak Tree Press.

Sweeney, P. (2001), "Ireland moves towards economic model of Manila" in *Irish Times*, 16 April 2001.

Tansey, P. (1998), *Ireland at Work: Economic Growth and the Labour Market, 1987–1997*, Dublin: Oak Tree Press.

United Nations (2001), *Human Development Report 2001*, New York: UNDP.

Urwin, D.W. (1989), *Western Europe since 1945: A Political History*, Harlow: Longman.

Walker, J. and Pettigrew, T.F. (1984), "Relative Deprivation Theory: An Overview and Conceptual Critique", *British Journal of Social Psychology*, Vol. 23, pp. 301–310.

Wallis, R. and Bruce, S. (1992), "Secularization: The Orthodox Model" in S. Bruce (ed.), *Religion and Modernization: Sociologists and Historians Debate the Secularization Thesis*, Oxford: Clarendon Press.

Waters, J. (1997), *An Intelligent Person' Guide to Modern Ireland*, London: Duckworth.

Waugh, E. (1968), *Brideshead Revisited*, Harlow: Longman.

Whelan, C.T. (ed.) (1994), *Values and Social Change in Ireland*, Dublin: Gill and Macmillan.

Wilson, B. (1966), *Religion in Secular Society*, London: Watts.

INDEX